Ph

C000135797

Disclaimer

All the content in this book is subject to copyright and may not be reproduced in any form without written consent of Pharmacy OnBoard. Description or reference to an organisation, product of publication or service does not imply endorsement of that, unless it is owned by the Pharmacy OnBoard team, in which case it is subject to the disclaimers and limitations of liability. While the Pharmacy OnBoard team strives to make the information in this book as timely and accurate as possible. The team makes no claims or guarantees about the accuracy or adequacy of the content and expressly disclaims liability for errors within stated content. Pharmacy OnBoard does not guarantee success in the registration assessment. The material in this book is intended for use an exam revision aid or personal development resource. It is not a substitute for your own judgement as a professional.

All the trademarks mentioned in this book are the property of their respective owners.

Contents

Preface

As I earned my degree in pharmacy, I began to recognize the imminent importance of pharmaceuticals for managing the health and well-being of everyone. In my years of practice, after watching the recovery of so many of my patients, I realized that my strategies could be used to help others.

In the United Kingdom, training to become a pharmacist incorporates the learning and demonstration of patient centred care in an integrated, holistic manner. Pharmacists primarily focus on people's individual health needs, but are also involved in auditing pharmacy services, managing teams and promoting health.

After completing four years of undergraduate studies, and another fifty-two weeks of pre-registration training. Every individual who sits the exam hopes that after all those years of hard work; that they do overcome the final hurdle. This book was designed to assist with exam practise, whilst providing practise of GPhC style clinical exam questions, exercises and case studies. The extract based questions have specifically been formulated to help you to navigate your way around external sources of various medicinal products to accurately answer exam questions. This book should be used as a revision aid to help increase your efficiency and exam performance.

Every individual sitting the registration exam, must remember that they are very intelligent and capable of passing the exam, because they have already achieved a master's degree in pharmacy. To get the positive results that candidates deserve, they must make a commitment to be positive. I know that you will be a great and successful pharmacist. Your hard work will pay off to achieve your dream.

All the best

Amit Luthra
The Pharmacy OnBoard team

Abbreviations

AC	Before food
ACBS	Advisory Committee on Borderline Substances, see Borderline Substances
ACE	Angiotensin-converting enzyme
ACEI	Angiotensin-converting enzyme inhibitor
ADHD	Attention deficit hyperactivity disorder
A & E	Accident and Emergency
AED	Anti-epileptic drugs
AF	Atrial fibrillation
AIDS	Acquired immunodeficiency syndrome
ALT	Alternative
AMP	Ampoule
Ante	Before
Applic	Apply
Approx.	Approximately
AUR	Appliance Use Review
AV	Atrioventricular
BAN	British Approved Name
BD	Twice daily
BMI	Body mass index
BNF	British National Formulary
BP	British Pharmacopoeia
BP	Blood pressure
BPM	Beats per minute
BPC	British Pharmaceutical Codex 1973
BRCA	Breast cancer gene
BSA	Body surface area
BTS	British Thoracic Society
cAMP	Cyclic adenosine monophosphate
CCG	Clinical Commissioning Group

CD	Controlled Drug
CD1	Controlled Drug in Schedule 1 of the Misuse of Drugs Regulations 2001
CD2	Controlled Drug in Schedule 2 of the Misuse of Drugs Regulations 2001
CD3	Controlled Drug in Schedule 3 of the Misuse of Drugs Regulations 2001
CD4 I	Controlled Drug in Schedule 4 (Part I) of the Misuse of Drugs Regulations 2001
CD4 II	Controlled Drug in Schedule 4 (Part II) of the Misuse of Drugs Regulations 2001
CD5	Controlled Drug in Schedule 5 of the Misuse of Drugs Regulations 2001
CFC	Chlorofluorocarbon
CHM	Commission on Human Medicines
CHMP	Committee for Medicinal Products for Human Use
CL-	Chloride ions
CNS	central nervous system
COX	Cyclooxygenase
COPD	Chronic obstructive pulmonary disease
CPPE	Centre for pharmacy postgraduate education
CrCl	Creatinine Clearance (mL/minute)
CSM	Committee on Safety of Medicines
CT	Computerized tomography
DMARD	Disease-modifying antirheumatic drug
DOAC	Direct oral anticoagulants
DPF	Dental Practitioners' Formulary
DPP-4	Dipeptidyl-peptidase 4
DT	Drug Tariff price
E/C	Enteric coated
ECG	Electrocardiogram
EEG	Electro-encephalogram
eGFR	Estimated glomerular filtration rate
EHC	Emergency hormonal contraception

ESR	Erythrocyte sedimentation rate
Extemp	Extemporaneously dispensed
FC	Film-coated
FORT	Strong
FSH	Follicle-stimulating hormone
FSRH	Faculty of Sexual and Reproductive Healthcare
FY1	Foundation Year 1
FY2	Foundation Year 2
G	Gram
GFR	Glomerular filtration rate
GIP	Glucose-dependent insulinotropic polypeptide
GLP-1	Glucagon-like peptide-1
GP	General practitioner
GPhC	General Pharmaceutical Council
GR	Gastro-resistant
GSL	General sales list
GTN	Glyceryl trinitrate
GTT	Drops
HbA1C	Glycated haemoglobin
HDL-cholesterol	high-density lipoprotein cholesterol
HIV	Human immunodeficiency virus
HR	Heart Rate
HRS	Hours
HRT	Hormone replacement therapy
IBS	Irritable bowel syndrome
IBW	Ideal Body Weight
ICS	Inhaled corticosteroid
IM	Intramuscular
INF	Infusion
INJ	Injection
IV	Intravenous

INR	International Normalised Ratio
IUD	Intrauterine Device
JCVI	Joint Committee on Vaccination and Immunisation
K+	Potassium ion
KG	Kilogram
LDL-cholesterol	Low-density lipoprotein cholesterol
L	Litre
LFT	Liver function test
LH	Luteinizing hormone
MANE	Morning
MAOI	Monoamine-oxidase inhibitor
Max	Maximum
MCV	mean corpuscular (CELL) volume
MDU	As directed
MDI	Metered dose inhaler
MEP	Medicines, Ethics and practice guide
MHRA	Medicines and Healthcare products Regulatory Agency
MIN	Minute
MITTE	Send
MG	Milligram
ML	Millilitre
MM	Millimetre
mmHG	Millimetre of mercury
MMR	Measles, mumps and rubella
MR	Modified release
MRI	Magnetic resonance imaging
MUR	Medicines use review
NCL	No cautionary label
NHS	National Health Service
NICE	National Institute for Health and Care Excellence

NMS	New Medicines Service
NOCTE	Night
NPF	Nurse Prescribers' Formulary
NRLS	National Reporting and Learning System
NSAID	Non-steroidal anti-inflammatory drug
NSTEMI	Non-ST-segment elevation myocardial infarction
OC	Oral contraception
OCU	Ocular application
OD	Every day
OM	Every morning
ON	Every night
OP	Original pack
ORT	Oral rehydration therapy
OTC	Over the counter
P	Pharmacy (only)
PA	To the affected area
PAST	Paste
PC	After food
PCT	Primary Care Trust
PEG	Percutaneous endoscopic gastrostomy
PGD	Patient Group Direction
PHE	Public Health England
PIL	Patient information leaflet
PMR	Patient medical record
POM	Prescription-only medication
POM-V	Prescription-only medication veterinarian
PPI	Proton pump inhibitor
PR	Per rectum
PRE-REG	Pre-registration pharmacist
PRN	When required
PT	Patient

QD	Four times daily
QDS	To be taken four times daily
QQH	Every fourth hour
QS	Sufficient
Q12H	Every 12 hours
QQ	Every
®	Trademark
rDNA	Ribosomal Deoxyribonucleic acid
RP	Responsible Pharmacist
RX	Prescription
S/C	sugar-coated
SC	Subcutaneous
SCR	Summary care record
SL	Sublingual
SLS	Selected List Scheme
SMC	Scottish Medicines Consortium
SOP	Standard operating procedure
SPC	Summary of Product Characteristics
SPP.	Species
SSRI	Selective serotonin reuptake inhibitor
STAT	Immediately
STEMI	ST-segment elevation myocardial infarction
TCA	Tricyclic antidepressant
TDD	Three times daily
TDS	To be taken three times daily
TPN	Total parenteral nutrition
TRIT	Serial dilution
TSH	Thyroid stimulating hormone
U&E	Urea and electrolytes
UK	United Kingdom
UTI	Urinary Tract Infection

UV	Ultraviolet
VTE	Venous thromboembolism
WFI	Water for injection
WHO	World Health Organization
WSP	White soft paraffin
W/V	Weight in volume
W/W	Weight in weight
YSP	Yellow Soft Paraffin

Introduction

The pharmacist is often the first healthcare professional that patients and the public will have contact with when seeking help. Thus, a pharmacist's role in this sector within the UK and NHS is vital. The responsibility is significantly more than just dispensing. As a pharmacist's role is becoming more and more clinical, this shift in changing role brings growth and development to pharmacy as a career.

Pharmacists who choose to follow pharmacy as a career, commit to life-long learning. To be able to effectively carry this out, continual professional development is vital, which fundamentally allows pharmacists to revaluate and assess their current knowledge. Pharmacists primarily direct patient care services in the community to promote health, wellness, and disease prevention.

Pharmacists are an integral part of the interdisciplinary approach at all levels of care for all healthcare settings, who collaborate with other healthcare workers to improve pharmaceutical care. The adept of knowledge that pharmacists have, is required to create and review comprehensive drug therapy plans for patients, identify and achieve optimum therapeutic goals and to review all prescribed medications prior to their dispensing and administration to the patient. Pharmacists must remain competent to ensure they safely evaluate the appropriateness of drug therapy (e.g., drug choice, dose, route, frequency, and duration of therapy).

Pass The Pharmacist Registration Exam has been specifically written following the GPhC registration exam framework. This book comprises of over 230 clinical questions. You may refer to reference sources, however all the questions comprise imminent information needed to derive an answer, to enable you to revise for your exam. The book incorporates clinical patient case studies that enables you to revise various areas of pharmacy practice and relate them to real case studies - as you may encounter in the GPhC assessment. All the questions follow the most current treatment guidelines at the time of writing. This volume should be practised under timed conditions. Pharmacy OnBoard has a panel of successful UK registered, practising pharmacists who each have invaluable experience in the training of pharmacists over the last decade. Each question has been carefully designed to test your knowledge and challenge your potential. Pharmacy OnBoard endeavours this to be used as a comprehensive revision aid, by pharmacy students and pharmacists to gain success.

For more updates on the latest events and revision aids from Pharmacy OnBoard, please visit our Instagram portal @pharmacy_onboard.

Feedback

Pharmacy OnBoard works alongside pharmacy students and pre-registration pharmacists in Great Britain. Established in 2014, the association aims to provide compressive preparatory material, support and assist trainees on their path towards registration.

As part of this supportive and representative role, Pharmacy OnBoard invited feedback following the publication of the highly successful first, second, third and fourth edition of 'Pass The Pharmacist Registration Exam'. As of 1st July 2019, 2897 respondents provided excellent feedback, through this Pharmacy OnBoard have been able to collate feedback, present it to the panel of successful UK registered, practising pharmacists. This was then reviewed and categorised into themes. The feedback included a number of recommendations, all of which were accepted to better the experience for our trainees and have led to improvements in the fifth edition of this book.

Pharmacy OnBoard hopes that this fifth edition is useful for all stakeholders, particularly the trainee pharmacists. Should you have any comments, please do not hesitate to contact us.

Exam technique

Over the past few years, Pharmacy OnBoard has been helping pre-registration pharmacists take the GPhC exam. We have compiled our top eight tips for gaining success with the pharmacist registration assessment.

1.   **To RELAX:** The pass rate varies every year, depending on the performance of students across the board. The pass mark is around 70%. Unnecessary stress and nervousness only lead to added pressure during the exam. Relaxation before exam is the key for better performance. Try to practice deep breathing to help calm the nerves. Go in with a calm mind and to enable better performance. Sleep early the night before and do not have a heavy breakfast prior to the exam.

2.   **To BELIEVE in yourself:** The registration assessment is not as hard as you think it is. The majority of the time, the mock assessment questions/courses are much more complicated than the real GPhC exam. This is only to ensure that you are better prepared for the assessment. So, if you pass the Pharmacy OnBoard questions with a 70% average, then you should expect an 80% average result in the actual exam.

3.   **To REVISE early:** Do not leave the revision for the exam until April/May time. It is important to ensure that towards the second half of the pre-registration year, you maintain consistency with the level of revision you undertake. Although, it is never too early to start revision. Our experience with pre-registration pharmacists, suggests that core revision should begin around January (around 6 months before the assessment). Ensure that you are familiar with the structure and layout of SPC'S, and PIL's which will increase your efficiency with extract questions. Resources such as the BNF, MEP, GPhC guidance documents should be thoroughly dissected and understood to ensure you have a solid grasp of the fundamental knowledge.

4.   **To familiarise with OTC sale restrictions:** Trainee pharmacists working in community pharmacy will have a greater exposure to the sale and supply of OTC medicine sale, than those who work in the hospital/GP or industry

sector. So, ensure, that you have some exposure to OTC licensing and sale requirements. Remember, the registration assessment doesn't discriminate between pharmacy sectors and will test your knowledge across the board through patient case scenarios. Spend some time gaining OTC experience.

5.   ***To understand pharmaceutical LAW:***
Understanding pharmacy law is not only necessary for passing the registration assessment but is needed beyond that to become a confident and competent pharmacist. It will allow you to get acquainted with all legal proceedings relevant to human and veterinary medicinal manufacturing, packing, distribution, imports, exports, sales, marketing, licensing and registration of the drugs/medicines and associated penalties.

6.   ***To practise TIME management:*** Practicing exam technique is the most important thing you can do, to learn how to finish the registration exam on-time. The most important part of time management is practice. You should commit to practising full mock exam papers under timed exam conditions. Managing your time in the GPhC assessment will take off so much pressure and will stop you making silly mistakes in a panic. Remember to break up the time in advance for each question and capitalise on the reading time for case scenarios. If you find you are dwelling on one question for too long, then move to the next question and return to it later.

7.   ***To practise CALCULATIONS:*** Our experience with pre-registration exam preparation suggests that consistent maths calculations practice should begin at least 3 months prior to the exam. Students should aim to carry out at least 4 pharmaceutical calculation questions per day of varying types, every day. This would ensure that, at least by the assessment day you would have practiced at least 336 different types of pharmaceutical calculation questions. Pharmacy OnBoard's calculation guide provides a vast range of these types of question.

8.   ***To use many RESOURCES:*** For success in the registration assessment, it is vital that you use reliable sources to revise from. The more resources used, the wider your knowledge base will be for the exam. The team at

Pharmacy OnBoard has designed MCQs which mirror the format of that in the registration assessment to allow testing and practice for a wide breadth of pharmaceutical content and objectives. This will provide with an objective measurement of your current and perspective ability.

Approach to Clinical Questions

Welcome to the Pharmacy OnBoard clinical questions book. This guide includes a whole range of different scenarios. You should work through these questions and then confirm your answers with the solutions provided at the back of this book. The first section of the book contains over 150 clinical MCQ's, followed by 50 simple pharmacy questions. The last section comprises of 20 YES / NO questions.

Pharmacy OnBoard have developed questions based on relevant clinical case studies, as found in the style and format of the GPhC registration assessment. Please note that our organisation is independent of the GPhC and questions have been developed to broaden your clinical knowledge and expose you a wide range of concepts expected to be known.

Make sure that you pay full attention to the style of questions. Distractors are commonly added to questions to deviate your concentration. It is vital, that as a pharmacist you are able to pick the key information out of the variety of parameters presented to you in a real-life patient scenario and then to make an appropriate clinical judgement as required. Our questions specifically have distractors incorporated in them to develop your confidence in dealing with them.

The journey to becoming a pharmacist is not an easy one. Clinical questions can be seen as either a hurdle or a form of passive love. Mastering your ability to do well in the clinical exam will lead you to the right way of success.

This booklet is designed to help develop your clinical understanding and support you; it contains questions at a lower grade to help your preparation. How you use this book depends on you, but Pharmacy OnBoard recommends that your prime focus is on your weakest areas to cultivate your competence before the registration assessment.

We recommend that you practice questions as much as possible within an environment that is free from distractions.

Once you are a qualified pharmacist or a pharmacy technician, as a professional you must take on the responsibility for your own work. You must ensure that you remain competent so that you can confidently practice throughout your time. To effectively do this, you must understand and work towards the expectations of the regulating body.

Self-study will direct your own learning so that you gain a grasp of handling different concepts. The questions outlined in this workbook by Pharmacy OnBoard combine a mixture of scenarios that may be seen in both outpatient and inpatient situations.

Evidence based practice must be implemented in education, so that learners appreciate its importance and are able to become competent to serve the community and influence behaviour in terms of decision-making, through application of an evidence based approach in professional practice. In essence, having this agenda would only further improve the quality of the healthcare service provision. While engaging all stakeholders including patients, healthcare professionals and trainers.

To practice as a healthcare professional as a newly qualified graduate can be quite daunting at first. Pharmacy is a very heavy content loaded vocation. Throughout your career, at some point you will be faced with exams and assessments. Regardless of whether you are an experienced senior or just a graduate. It is vital that you develop good habits right from the beginning.

Planning ahead will help you to critically analyse the availability of time and resources you have and to prioritise that. This could be used to ensure that you have adequate amounts of time to cover several revision topics over a certain time period and avoid cramming. You cannot expect to cram for pharmacy exams, there is just too much content. Revising little but often would ensure you are not overwhelmed when exam season approaches.

Remember, in a subject like pharmacy, the amount of content around drug pharmacology is so vast that it is almost impossible to learn every single bit of detail. So, a top tip is that breadth of knowledge is important, not depth. As a pharmacy student, it is better to know a little bit about all of your topics than learn one particular topic or drug in great detail, as this will not help you to perform well in clinical pharmacology exams. Especially when there is a time constraint on revision time. Having a broader understanding would be practically more beneficial.

Active revision is a skill you must exercise. Re-reading notes cannot be classed as high quality, effective revision. You must actively question your strengths and weaknesses when recalling facts or knowledge from a subject that you have prepared for. Just going through something once and leaving it till the exam will not be enough to create a cognitive imprint. You could use brain storms, flash cards, MCQ's to reinforce what you learnt. Constantly revising can be bad for you also, regular breaks are important. Passing exams is important, but so should be the process of revision.

Malaria

Malaria prophylaxis tablets can sometimes be pre-calculated on prescriptions or may require you as the pharmacist to calculate the final quantity of tablets required to dispense.

- *Based on an adult dose Proguanil is given as 2 tablets/day*
- *Based on an adult dose Chloroquine is given as 2 tablets/week*

Age: (years)	Proguanil hydrochloride 100 mg (DAILY)	Chloroquine phosphate 250 mg tablets (WEEKLY)
1 to 4	Half a tablet	Half a tablet
5 to 8	One tablet	One tablet
9 to 14	One and half tablet	One and half tablet
14+	Two tablets	Two tablets
Both medications must be taken 1 week before travelling to high-risk malaria area, the duration of travel, then 4 weeks on return.		
Thus, someone travelling on holiday for 1 weeks would require a total of 6 weeks treatment.		
Thus, someone travelling on holiday for 2 weeks would require a total of 7 weeks treatment.		

Inhalers

Each inhaler preparation contains varying ingredients, quantities of puffs and doses. You may be given an extract along with the question for the product or the relevant information may be supplied in the question. Questions on inhalers would usually require you to calculate the duration of therapy, the total number of puffs, quantity of active drug or the sum of inhalers required.

- To find out the total amount of drug in an inhaler:
Multiply the total number of doses by the strength of that inhaler.
- To find out the total quantity of inhalers to supply:
Multiply the total number of puffs by the overall duration of treatment, be vary of the units.

Creatinine Clearance

$$\text{Estimated Creatinine Clearance in mL/minute} = \frac{(140 - \text{Age}) \times \text{Weight} \times \text{Constant}}{\text{Serum creatinine}}$$

- Age of the patient would be in years.
- Weight of the patient would be in kilograms.

However ideal body weight maybe required for those patients who are majorly underweight or overweight.

- Patient's serum creatinine levels would be in micromole/litre
- Constant: 1.23 for males
- Constant: 1.04 for females

Primarily, creatinine clearance (CrCl) would be described as the volume of blood plasma creatinine that clears through the kidneys over time. This parameter is an inexpensive and efficient way of determining renal functional state. When assessing a patient, creatinine clearance and glomerular filtration rate (GFR) are both correlative components that help establish levels of creatinine in blood and urine filtrate.

With patients who have a body mass index (BMI) less than $18\,\text{kg/m}^2$ or greater than $40\,\text{kg/m}^2$, then, when calculating the CrCl or GFR, the calculation should be adjusted so that the ideal body weight is used as a parameter to adjust appropriately. As in such cases the patient's lean body mass is different from the actual body weight.

Clinical Questions

1. You are carrying out a health review for a patient in the pharmacy. The patient's blood pressure reading in clinic was XX/XX mmHg. You determined her to have stage 2 hypertension. Which of the following blood pressure reading could the patient have had?
   A) 152/106 mmHg
   B) 148/98 mmHg
   C) 185/122 mmHg
   D) 142/77 mmHg
   E) 191/120 mmHg

2. Mr LK, an 82 year old male patient would like general advice about hypertension. He currently only takes vitamin supplements to aid his progressing arthritis in his weight bearing joints. Mr LK is worried that he may develop hypertension due to his age as he has a family history of hypertension. He wants to know what should be the upper target for his blood pressure. Which of the following would you state?
   A) 120/80 mmHg
   B) 130/80 mmHg
   C) 140/90 mmHg
   D) 150/90 mmHg
   E) 160/100 mmHg

3. Miss CV, a 24 year old female has had mild hypertension over the past 39-weeks. Today she has given birth to her first child. Over the course of her pregnancy her hypertension was controlled by Methyldopa, 500mg BD. You have just finished reviewing her medication and Miss CV tells you

that she shall not be breastfeeding her child. What course of action should you take?

A) Advice Miss CV to continue taking the Methyldopa until her GP invites her for an annual blood pressure review.

B) Advice Miss CV to continue taking the Methyldopa for 14 days post-delivery and then to stop and get switched over to an alternative antihypertensive.

C) Advice Miss CV to continue taking the Methyldopa for 7 days post-delivery and then to stop and get switched over to an alternative antihypertensive.

D) Advice Miss CV to continue taking the Methyldopa for 5 days post-delivery and then to stop and get switched over to an alternative antihypertensive.

E) Advice Miss CV to discontinue taking the Methyldopa 2 days after giving birth and get switched over to an alternative antihypertensive.

4. In the outpatients hypertension clinic that you are running today. Miss FV, a 32 year old patient who has given birth to her third child about 6 months ago would like to talk to you about managing her hypertension. She is currently breast feeding. She tells you that after reading online about medications testing and trials, she has found that not many medications undergo testing on women who are pregnant or breast feeding. She has stage 2 hypertension, which cannot be managed by lifestyle intervention alone. Which of the following medications are suitable as first-line for a patient who is breast feeding postpartum?

A) Amlodipine 5mg OM

B) Diltiazem MR 240mg BD

C) Enalapril 20mg OD

D) Amiloride 10mg OD

E) Losartan 50mg OD

5. Mr UY is a 44 year old Caucasian male who had been diagnosed as having stage 1 hypertension last year. He has been taking Ramipril 5mg OM to manage the hypertension, he is on no other medications, however has chronic heart failure which is managed with a fluid restricted diet. Despite an increase in his Ramipril dose, his blood pressure has not been very stable lately and rather high, which his most recent clinic reading being at 152/99 mmHg. You are considering to add another antihypertensive drug to his treatment, to help with his blood pressure control. Which of the following would be most suited to start Mr UY on?

A) Angiotensin converting enzyme inhibitor

B) Angiotensin receptor blocker

C) Calcium channel blocker

D) Thiazide-like diuretic

E) Aldosterone antagonist

6. Mrs SF is a 65 year old female of Indian origin, she has an immediate family history of hypertension and has recently had an in clinic reading of 148/95 mmHg. The doctor would like to initiate Mrs SF on an antihypertensive, what would be the recommended first line treatment for her?

A) Ramipril 2.5mg tablet

B) Amlodipine 5mg tablet

C) Spironolactone 25mg tablet

D) Bendroflumethiazide 2.5mg tablet

E) Losartan 25mg tablet

7. You are running a study session at the local university with pharmacy undergraduate students on disorders related to pregnancy. You are asked about pre-eclampsia, which of the following would best describe its aetiology?
   A) **Characterized by the onset of severe low blood pressure.**
   B) **Characterized by the onset of high blood pressure.**
   C) **Characterized by the onset of dangerously low plasma sodium levels.**
   D) **Characterized by the onset of chronic hyperglycaemia.**
   E) **Characterized by the onset of gestational diabetes.**

8. Mrs CF a 29 year old female has gestational diabetes which is being managed effectively. The patient has now been diagnosed with having pre-eclampsia, which requires urgent pharmacological treatment. Which of the following is recommended as a first line treatment for her newly diagnosed condition?
   A) **Metformin**
   B) **Enalapril**
   C) **Labetalol**
   D) **Sodium Chloride**
   E) **Bisoprolol**

9. Mr YV has called the pharmacy seeking advice, he tells you that his doctor has informed him that Mr YV is at risk of developing stage 1 hypertension due to his 2 recent 'in clinic' sub-therapeutic readings. Mr YV has now been referred to you to gain some dietary and lifestyle advice about how he can have a healthier lifestyle. Which one of the following would you recommend?

    A) The patient must aim to consume no more than 2.4 grams of sodium chloride per day.

    B) The patient must aim to consume at least 14 units of alcohol per week.

    C) The patient must aim to consume no more than 6 grams of sodium chloride per day.

    D) The patient must aim to have a body mass index of at least 28.

    E) Mild hypertension cannot be controlled by diet and lifestyle interventions.

10. You are presented with a prescription for drug X to be dispensed for oral administration. You ask the patient whether they have used it before. The patient explains that this is a new oral medication, they have been issued by their doctor to manage his psoriasis which has now formed pustules. Which of the following could drug X be?

    A) Fluconazole

    B) Ciclosporin

    C) Gentamicin

    D) Tacrolimus

    E) Coal tar

11. Mrs LT, a 32 year old female who has been prescribed a new medication to prevent reoccurrence of her rheumatic fever. The patient tells you that when she was a child, she suffered from a scarlet fever infection, that was not treated properly, which developed into rheumatic fever. She states that her prescriber has given her this new medication as a prophylactic measure. Which of the following could this medication be?

A) Hydroxyzine

B) Sulfadiazine

C) Sulfinpyrazone

D) Sulfasalazine

E) Febuxostat

12. On the Obstetrics unit, a 21 year-old female with no significant past medical history presented with symptoms suggestive of a particular condition. Clinical manifestation included weight loss, mood changes and heat intolerance, with a decrease in concentration. Her immediate family history is significant for thyroid disease in both parents requiring adjunct thyroid replacement therapies. The consultant looking after the patient, has requested for thyroid function tests. Shortly after the results came, the patient was started on Carbimazole. What condition would the patient must likely have?

A) Hypercalcaemia

B) Hypoparathyroidism

C) Hypoglycaemia

D) Hyperthyroidism

E) Hypothyroidism

13. Following on from the previous question, you are the clinical pharmacist in the ward round and are carrying out medicines reconciliation for patients. You notice that Carbimazole is not suitable for the 21 year old patient. Why would this be?

    A) Obesity

    B) Immediate familial history

    C) The patient is under the age of 30 years

    D) Hypersensitivity

    E) Gestation

14. After carrying out the medicines reconciliation, you discuss the matter with the consultant on duty. Who advices to switch over the patient from Carbimazole to an alternative agent. Which of the following would be most appropriate for the patient?

    A) Propylthiouracil

    B) Patisiran

    C) Primidone

    D) Propranolol

    E) Pyridoxine

15. A clinical case study is being reviewed amongst the multidisciplinary team about a patient. A 44-year-old African woman with a benign Osteochondroma in her left knee presented to the emergency department, with a 3-day history of intractable nausea and vomiting. The patient experienced chest pain, palpitations, shortness of breath, tremor with sweating, disorientation and marked tachycardia. Her medical history included depression and anxiety with recent unexplained weight loss. The patient's medications included citalopram and paracetamol. On presentation, she

was febrile to 40.1°C, tachycardic to 154 BPM, and blood pressure was stable at 122/77mmHg. An urgent blood profile was requested. What is the most likely diagnosis?

A) Cushing's disease

B) Gestation

C) Hypothyroid (Hashimoto's disease)

D) Hyperglycaemia

E) Hyperthyroid (Thyroid storm)

16. You receive a call from your local GP practice. On the phone is the general practitioner asking advice about bulk prescribing. Which of the following statements best describe the process of bulk prescribing?

A) A bulk prescription is an order for several patients within a particular institute, for the treatment of more than one patient, they are looked after by a particular doctor that is responsible. Prescription Only Medicines (POMs) cannot be prescribed on bulk prescriptions.

B) A bulk prescription is an order for several patients within a particular institute, for the treatment of more than one patient, they are looked after by a particular doctor that is responsible. Controlled drugs can be prescribed on bulk prescriptions.

C) A bulk prescription is an order for one patient within a particular institute, for the treatment of more than one condition. General sales list (GSL) medications cannot be prescribed on bulk prescriptions.

D) A bulk prescription is an order for several patients within a particular institute, for the treatment of more than one patient, they are looked after by a particular doctor that is responsible. Prescription Only Medicines (POMs) can be prescribed on bulk prescriptions.

E) A bulk prescription is for a patient within a care home, for the treatment of more than one medical condition, they are looked after by a particular doctor that is responsible. Prescription Only Medicines (POMs) can be prescribed on bulk prescriptions.

17. What information about bulk prescriptions is incorrect?

A) A bulk prescription can be written or printed on an ordinary FP10 prescription

B) No prescription charge is payable when a bulk prescription is dispensed

C) The total quantity required for all residents on this medication

D) The bulk prescription must include: The wording *'for patients under my care at {the name of the care home}'*

E) Bulk prescriptions can be electronically transmitted

18. What of the following medication can be bulk prescribed?

A) **Lactulose syrup**

B) **Vitamin D tablets**

C) **Senna tablets**

D) **Paracetamol tablets**

E) **Domperidone tablets**

19. There have been several advantages listed by the Royal Pharmaceutical Society for bulk prescribing. Which of the following is not a benefit of bulk prescribing?

A) **Has the potential to reduce waste**

B) **Saves the NHS money**

C) **Potentially reduces excessive contamination of multiple packs**

D) **Reduces drug dispensing time**

E) **Saves RX paper**

20. A middle aged female has come in to purchase a bottle or oral Paracetamol suspension, you are counselling her about the dose that she should administer to her grandchild. What dose is most appropriate of Paracetamol for a 3-year old child?

A. **60 mg to be given every 4-6 hours**

B. **120 mg to be given every 4-6 hours**

C. **180 mg to be given every 4-6 hours**

D. **240 mg to be given every 4-6 hours**

E. **360 mg to be given every 4-6 hours**

21. You are a clinical pharmacist. Mr AL, is a medical student, who is completing a placement in a local hospital. They are working with you today on ward rounds. The consultant, is talking to a patient whilst writing her a prescription for an antibiotic, which a nurse will then administer. The consultant then receives an urgent request to go to the emergency department and leaves the ward. Mr AL has come to you to explain that he has reviewed the notes and realised that the patient is allergic to the antibiotic prescribed by the consultant. What would be the best course of action to take?

   A) Inform the senior nurse of this matter

   B) Review the patient medications and get an alternative prescribed

   C) Write a formal complaint about the consultant

   D) Converse with the patient

   E) Ignore the matter as the consultant knows what is best

22. Mr DW has come into the pharmacy. He would like to show the pharmacist his rash, so you take him into the consulting room. The rash starts centrally in the lower-right region of his chest, and follows a line around his body to the upper back. This rash then terminates just below his left armpit. After further questioning, you find that there are fluid filled blisters present across the body that are accompanied with a sharp pain, "like needles being poked". The symptoms are typical of which one of the following conditions?

   A. Dermatitis

   B. Bacterial impetigo

   C. Tinea unguingam

   D. Acne rosacea

   E. Shingles

23. The trainee pharmacist is asking for you to explain the meaning of clinical governance and its importance in community pharmacy. Which of the following is not part of clinical governance?

   A. **Clinical Auditing**

   B. **Standards of practice**

   C. **Education and training of staff**

   D. **Human Resources within the pharmacy**

   E. **Managing risk management**

24. Miss WP, has started sulfasalazine tablets, to take 1g four times a day for the initial treatment and management of her Crohns disease. Which of the listed adverse drug reaction does the patient need to be counselled about?

   A. **Myopathy**

   B. **QT interval prolongation**

   C. **Reduced eGFR**

   D. **Chest palpitations**

   E. **Sore throat**

25. Mrs VP has begun to take Pioglitazone 15mg OD for her type 2 diabetes, this is in addition to Metformin 1000mg TDS which has been tolerated well. She has been worried lately about her worsening of diabetic symptoms. You are dispensing Pioglitazone for the patient and are questioned about any adverse effects. Which of the following would Mrs VP need to be made aware of?

   A. **Bradycardia**

   B. **Drowsiness**

   C. **Haematuria**

D. Hypertensive crisis

E. Hypertension

26. An 83 year old patient who has been taking Atorvastatin 40mg at night, Lisinopril 10mg daily with Atenolol 100mg daily, has now had the dose of his statin increased to 80mg daily. Upon counselling the patient, which of the listed adverse reactions should the patient look out for?

A) Haematuria

B) Low mood

C) Myopathy

D) QT interval prolongation

E) Alopecia

27. You are clinically assessing a patients notes, he is of 83 years of age and takes Co-Beneldopa to manage his Parkinson's disease and has had his dose recently increased. His notes state that this dose change has aggravated his nausea for which his GP has commenced Domperidone. Which side-effect should the patient monitor?

A) Endocarditis

B) Hypotension

C) Vitiligo

D) QT interval prolongation

E) Gingival hyperplasia

28. Mr HS has been commenced on Warfarin last week for the prevention of stroke and MI. He has already been diagnosed with atrial fibrillation. Whilst counselling you explain to the patient that under-anticoagulation can lead to thrombosis and over-

anticoagulation to bleeding. Mr HS asks, which side-effect he should look out for?

A) Hypoglycaemia

B) Decreased concentration

C) Haematuria

D) Hypertension

E) Dermatitis

29. A trainee nurse has come to the pharmacy department seeking help on an exam question she was attempting. The question is asking about the mechanism of action of drugs. Which of the drug listed is a direct selective factor XA inhibitor, which interrupts the intrinsic and extrinsic pathway?

A) Warfarin

B) Doxazosin

C) Lisinopril

D) Rivaroxaban

E) Ticagrelor

30. Today you are carrying out structured medication reviews for patients in the blood pressure clinic. You are reviewing Mr IP's drugs, he has recently started a new medication but complains of weight gain. You notice from the recorded observations that your patient has had significant weight gain over the last month, with no peripheral oedema. Which drug listed is most likely to be responsible?

A. Amlodipine

B. Metronidazole

C. Metformin

D. Bisoprolol

E. Doxazosin

31. A middle-aged male has come into your pharmacy looking to purchase sun creams and travel plugs. Your healthcare advisor is offering him advice on how to keep safe as he is travelling to Dubai for a holiday and has sensitive skin. The patient then informs the pharmacy advisor that he is currently on several medications and is concerned if they will interact with the sun cream? You review his PMR and find that although not an interaction, one of his medications can cause photosensitivity reactions? Which medication is this?

   A) **Amlodipine**

   B) **Bendroflumethiazide**

   C) **Amiodarone**

   D) **Candesartan**

   E) **Atorvastatin**

32. Mr SD has come into the pharmacy requesting to purchase some Pholcodine. Unfortunately, your pharmacy is out of stock today and you are unable to supply the patient with it. You question the patient on the type of cough they have, to determine if an alternative cough mixture would be suitable. Mr SD tells you that he has a persistent dry cough which is really frustrating him. It wakes him up at night and has got worse since he started a new medication. Which of the drug listed below is most likely to be responsible for this?

   A) **Lisinopril**

   B) **Doxazosin**

   C) **Losartan**

   D) **Clopidogrel**

   E) **Aspirin**

33. In the stroke clinic, you are reviewing patient's medications. Patient X has been prescribed a new medication for prevention of an atherothrombotic event. Which of the drug listed would be prescribed together with aspirin for a period of 12 months?

    A. Candesartan

    B. Febuxostat

    C. Alteplase

    D. Rivaroxaban

    E. Ticagrelor

34. The medicines optimisation team at your hospital trust are producing training material for the new trainee pharmacists. One of the posters is intended to simplify the side effects that antibiotics may cause. This particular poster mentions different drugs may affect the colour of urine. Which one of the following drugs change the colour of urine to orange-red after ingestion?

    A. Phenoxymethylpenicillin

    B. Clarithromycin

    C. Metronidazole

    D. Oxytetracycline

    E. Rifampicin

35. A 63-year-old female has been booked into your outpatients' stroke clinic. She has no significant past medical history apart from atrial fibrillation. The patient had suffered from a TIA 7 months ago but has managed well since then. The patient would not like to undergo cardioversion at this stage. The patients' other parameters are unremarkable such as blood pressure, inflammatory markers and FBC. If this patient

remains in a chronic state of atrial fibrillation, what would be the most therapeutic treatment to offer?

A) Phytomenadione

B) Warfarin

C) Heparin

D) Dipyridamole

E) Ticagrelor

36. You are reviewing the local trusts medication formulary. Patient X has a penicillin allergy, he requires treatment as he is suffering from an upper respiratory tract infection (URTI), which of the antibiotics stated would be most appropriate for a patient suffering from a URTI?

A) Sodium Fusidate

B) Gentamicin

C) Clarithromycin

D) Cefuroxime

E) Co-Amoxiclav

37. You are counselling a newly diagnosed diabetic. The patient asks if there are particular foods, he should carry with himself while travelling. Which of the following would you recommend, especially for use during a hypoglycaemic attack?

A) Carbonated water

B) Diet Lemonade

C) Kale salad

D) Sweets

E) Crisps

38. The counter assistant is providing advice to a woman currently in her third trimester of pregnancy. Which of the vitamin stated below should the pregnancy woman avoid during her period of gestation?

A) **Vitamin B12**

B) **Iron**

C) **Folic acid**

D) **Vitamin A**

E) **Vitamin D**

39. A teenage male is seeking advice about vitamin deficiency. He tells you that he has recently completed his GCSE exams but has been experiencing a dull and achy pain in both his wrists. After a blood test his GP has diagnosed him with Rickets. Which of the following vitamin deficiency may cause Rickets?

A. **Vitamin A**

B. **Vitamin C**

C. **Vitamin D**

D. **Vitamin E**

E. **Vitamin K**

40. You receive a phone call to your pharmacy from a woman wanting some advice on which product to purchase for her baby. She explains that her baby screams a lot at night and cries extensively. Furthermore, the baby's abdomen is rather tensed, and arms are quite stiff. What could the baby be experiencing from?

A) **Neonatal jaundice**

B) **Colic**

C) **Anaemia**

D) Otitis media

E) Tinea capitis

41. After discussing the matter with the patient's mother over the phone, you determine a diagnosis. You offer her some lifestyle advice; however, she has tried most of the advice you gave already. In this instance, which of the following medication is licensed for infantile colic?

A. Acetylsalicylic acid

B. Alginic acid

C. Bismuth

D. Simethicone

E. Aluminium hydroxide

42. In your pharmacy today, a lady has come in to purchase something OTC. You can see that the lady is heavily pregnant, she is suffering from constipation and is on no other medication and has no other medical conditions. Which of the following OTC preparation would be suitable for you to recommend to this patient?

A. Senna tablets

B. Bisacodyl tablets

C. Codeine phosphate

D. Lactulose syrup

E. Enoxaparin

You are carrying out a training session with foundation year-2 junior doctors about drug pharmacokinetics and ADME processes. Towards the end of the session, you are asked questions about different medications and their contraindications. The following four questions about different patients relate to the 5 options listed below, please choose the most appropriate answer.

A) **Asthma**

B) **Product of tp-RNA**

C) **Diabetes Mellitus**

D) **Hypoglycaemia**

E) **Pregnancy**

F) **Recombinant DNA technology**

G) **Mania associated with bipolar disorder**

From the options above, please select the most appropriate answer:

43. A patient was administered a dose of Misoprostol for the termination of her pregnancy. Which condition stated above would contraindicate the use of Misoprostol?

44. Quetiapine is used to treat which one of the above condition?

45. What is Glargine a product of?

46. Which condition may require assessment of peripheral organs for damage?

47. Methadone is an opioid analgesic, it is licensed for use in moderate to severe pain that has not responded to other first-line analgesics, or as an alternative for pain that is unresponsive. Methadone has also commonly been used in palliative care as an analgesic or alternatively in treating patients with drug dependence or opioid-tolerance as they may not respond to traditional regimens. Which of the following statements are correct about methadone?

A) Methadone should only be administered once daily due to risk of accumulation.

B) Hyperhidrosis is not a common side effect experienced when taking Methadone.

C) Methadone is a long-acting opioid.

D) ECG monitoring is not required for those patients maintained on Methadone.

E) The dose of Methadone must be increased when administered to those patients who have hypothyroidism.

48. You have a male and female, who are both in their early 20's asking to seek some advice about contraception. They have been advised to use effective contraception as one of them are on a medication which has one of the following effects. Which effect could this be?

A) Sedative

B) Teratogenic

C) Sympathomimetic

D) Parasympathetic

E) Increases seizure potential

49. You have a query over the phone about combined oral contraceptives. The nurse wants to enquire about monophasic and multiphasic contraceptives that are available. Which of the following statement is true?

A) A multiphasic combined oral contraceptive would have fixed amounts of oestrogen and progestogen in each active tablet.

B) A monophasic combined oral contraceptive would have different amounts of oestrogen and a progestogen in each active tablet.

C) A monophasic combined oral contraceptive would have a fixed amount of oestrogen only in each active tablet.

D) A multiphasic combined oral contraceptive would have varied amount of oestrogen and progestogen in each active tablet.

E) A multiphasic combined oral contraceptive would have varying amounts of oestrogen, progestogen and norethisterone in each tablet.

50. Combined hormonal contraceptive regimens are available as 21-day or 28-day preparations. Out of the two forms, the 21-day regimen contains 21 active birth control pills, whereas the 28-day form contains 21 active pills and 7 placebo pills. The patient seeking effective contraception must take the active pill for 21 consecutive days. Prescribers can prescribe contraceptives for up to 12 months per supply for hormonal contraception. However, it is vital that patients are regularly reviewed annually. Which of the following must clinicians not need to review annually for a patient on oral hormonal contraceptives?

A) Blood pressure

B) Plasma glycaemic control

C) Body mass index

D) Concomitant use of medications

E) Body weight

51. Mrs. PL is a 32-year-old female patient who has been maintained on a monophasic combined hormonal contraceptive pill for several years. In the next 6 weeks, Mrs PL is scheduled to undergo a cosmetic procedure on her abdomen and lower torso. Her consultant has advised that she will be immobile for at least 2 weeks after the surgery and will be considered for adequate thromboprophylaxis. Does the patient need to stop any of her medications prior to surgery?

    A) **Mrs PL can continue using her combined oral contraceptive pill as normal as she is not obese.**

    B) **Mrs PL must stop using her combined oral contraceptive pill at least 1 week before the elective surgery.**

    C) **Mrs PL must stop using her combined oral contraceptive pill at least 2 weeks before the elective surgery.**

    D) **Mrs PL must stop using her combined oral contraceptive pill at least 4 weeks before the elective surgery.**

    E) **Mrs PL must stop using her combined oral contraceptive pill at least 8 weeks before the elective surgery.**

52. The progestogen-only pill prevents pregnancy by thickening the mucosal layer in the cervix, thus prevents sperm from easily penetrating. Which of the following is not an example of a progestogen that is available as an active ingredient in a progestogen only contraceptive?

    A) **Levonorgestrel**

    B) **Noethisterone**

    C) **Desogestral**

D) Etonogestral

E) Estrone

53. Medroxyprogesterone is an example of a parenteral progestogen only contraceptive which is administered every 13 weeks to those wanting highly effective contraception. Which of the following counselling points are false?

A. **This form of contraception is not routinely used as first line for those patients who are over the age of 50 years.**

B. **Progestogen only preparations are associated with loss of bone mineral density.**

C. **After discontinuation of a depot medroxyprogesterone acetate injection, female fertility is not returned for at least a year after.**

D. **Patients who have osteoporosis should consider alternative progestogen only preparations.**

E. **Medroxyprogesterone is contraindicated in those patients who have a history of thromboembolism**

54. Miss WR is a 17-year-old female patient who has been taking a combined oral contraceptive for the past 14 months without any issues. Last week she was diagnosed with generalized epilepsy associated with Tonic-Clonic seizures. The patient has been initiated on Carbamazepine 100mg OD tablets and will be closely monitored until her next review with the consultant. She has been referred to you to optimize usage of her other medications. Which of the following would be the best course of action for you to take?

A. As Carbamazepine is an enzyme inhibitor, the plasma concentration of her oral contraceptive would be increased. Thus, the dose must be altered.

B. As the patient is only being initiated on Carbamazepine, she does not need to do anything.

C. As Carbamazepine is an enzyme inducer, the plasma concentration of her oral contraceptive would be decreased. Miss WR should be advised to change to a more reliable contraceptive method that would be unaffected by the Carbamazepine such as parenteral progestogen-only contraceptives or intra-uterine devices.

D. Advice the patient to use a monophasic combined oral contraceptive. This would have to be at a dose of 50 micrograms or more daily of ethinylestradiol. This must be used on a tricycling regimen without a break followed by a shortened tablet-free interval of four days.

E. Miss WR should be switched over to take Ulipristal acetate as a long-term contraceptive along with Carbamazepine. As enzyme inducers do not affect Ulipristal acetates plasma concentration.

55. Miss YT, is a 22-year-old female patient who has come into your pharmacy seeking to purchase emergency hormonal contraception. After carrying out a comprehensive consultation, you determine that she requires Ulipristal acetate and make the sale to her. Miss YT then asks you about starting on regular contraception from tomorrow as she does not want to keep purchasing emergency pills as they are expensive. How do you respond?

A. **Miss YT can start using regular hormonal contraception; however, this must only be started 5 days after taking the Ulipristal acetate tablet today.**

B. **Miss YT can start using regular hormonal contraception, from the next consecutive day after taking the Ulipristal acetate tablet today.**

C. **Miss YT does not need to use any contraception for this cycle, as the emergency Ulipristal tablet has protected her from pregnancy until her next cycle.**

D. **Miss YT can start using regular hormonal contraception 12 hours after taking the Ulipristal acetate tablet today.**

E. **After taking Ulipristal, Miss YT cannot use a progestogen only contraceptive in the same cycle and must wait until her next cycle begins, to commence hormonal contraception.**

56. A female in her late 30's has come to the pharmacy counter today, she is very confused and upset. She would like your advice and asks to speak with you in private. You take her to the consultation room; she tells you that she recently had an ectopic pregnancy and underwent a Salpingostomy, 3 days ago. Last night she was very stressed and ended up having unprotected intercourse with her regular partner. She is worried that she may be pregnant. Does she need emergency contraception?

A. The patient does not need any contraception, as she was treated for her ectopic pregnancy 3 days ago, she is still within the 5-day period of not requiring emergency contraception.

B. The patient must be supplied with a dose of Ulipristal acetate as her procedure was over 48 hours ago, she now requires emergency contraception.

C. The patient must be supplied with a dose of Levonorgestrel as her procedure was over 48 hours ago, she now requires emergency contraception.

D. After being treated for an ectopic pregnancy, the patient is not at risk of getting pregnant for at least 7 days post-procedure, she does not require contraception.

E. After being treated for an ectopic pregnancy, the patient is not at risk of getting pregnant for at least 10 days post-procedure, she does not require contraception.

57. Today is a Wednesday afternoon. A woman in her late 20's approaches you at the pharmacy and asks to purchase an emergency hormonal contraceptive. She tells you that is a Type-1 Diabetic and has recently had a gastric band fitted to help her lose weight, as currently she is morbidly obese with a body weight of 146kg and BMI 38 kg/m^2. You question her further to be able to make a safe and effective supply. She tells you that she had unprotected intercourse on Monday morning and although her partner did wear a condom, it ended up splitting. She is on no other medications apart from a short acting insulin which she uses for her glycaemic control. What should you do as the pharmacist? Choose the best option below.

A) Sell her Levonorgestrel as the intercourse was within 72 hours ago.

B) As the patient is obese, you must supply her with 2 Levonorgestrel tablets for effective contraception.

C) Refer the patient to the nearest sexual health clinic as you cannot make a supply of any OTC emergency contraceptive to her.

D) Make a sale of Ulipristal acetate to the patient as a form of emergency contraception, as the intercourse was within the 120-hour period.

E) As the patient is a Type-1 Diabetic, all forms of OTC emergency contraceptives are contraindicated, thus she must be referred to her GP. You cannot make a supply.

58. You are working at your local community pharmacy as a locum pharmacist, covering the shift for the regular store pharmacist who is off sick today. Mr DG, a 32-year-old male has come in seeking to purchase an iron supplement for himself, he asks to purchase the strongest strength that is available. Which of the following statements would be the best response?

A) Ask Mr DG, if he has had any Iron deficiency anaemia signs and symptoms. If he has, then offer to sell him Ferrous Sulphate 200mg tablets, one to be taken TDS.

B) Ask Mr DG, if he has had any Iron deficiency anaemia signs and symptoms. If he has, then offer to sell him Ferrous Gluconate 300mg tablets, one to be taken BD.

C) Ask Mr DG, if he has had any Iron deficiency anaemia signs and symptoms. If he has, then offer to sell him Ferrous Fumarate 210mg tablets, one to be taken BD.

D) Ask Mr DG, if he has had any Iron deficiency anaemia signs and symptoms. If he has, then offer to sell him Sodium Federate solution, one 5mL spoonful to be taken TDS.

E) Ask Mr DG, if he has had any Iron deficiency anaemia signs and symptoms. If he has, then signpost him to see his GP, or a medical practitioner to exclude any serious underlying cause of the anaemia.

59. Mr DG asks you what the average elemental dose of iron should be for an adult with an acute iron-deficiency?

    A) **10mg to 50mg of elemental iron daily**

    B) **50mg to 100mg of elemental iron daily**

    C) **100mg to 200mg of elemental iron daily**

    D) **300mg to 500mg of elemental iron daily**

    E) **500mg to 1000mg of elemental iron daily**

60. You are questioned further about the efficacy, absorption, and bioavailability of iron supplementation. Which of the following agents can increase the absorption and latter bioavailability of iron when taken together?

    A) **Lactic Acid**

    B) **Phosphoric Acid**

    C) **Ascorbic Acid**

    D) **Carbonic Acid**

    E) **Folic Acid**

61. The trainee pharmacist trainee is intrigued about the different formulations of iron that are available. They have been reading about Ferric Carboxymaltose, which is available as 1000mg/20ml solution for injection vials for parenteral use. The trainee asks you about switching over between different formulations of iron, which of the following statements is true?

    A) **Parenteral iron therapy is only used to treat and manage functional iron deficiency. Therefore, a patient requiring parenteral iron supplementation would not require any other form of iron supplementation.**

B) For a patient who may have been maintained on parenteral iron supplementation and now requires to be switched over to an oral iron formulation. Oral iron should not be given until 5 days after the last iron injection.

C) Parenteral iron formulations are not licensed to be used during gestation; only oral preparation can be used.

D) For a patient who may have been maintained on parenteral iron supplementation and now requires to be switched over to an oral iron formulation. Oral iron should not be given until 3 days after the last iron injection.

E) Patients of childbearing age who may intend to conceive a child should avoid using parenteral iron, as they do impair fertility.

62. After some time, Mr DG has come into your pharmacy again. This time he is presenting you with a prescription for a 2-month supply of iron tablets for himself. After the dispensing process is complete, you counsel Mr DG on taking this medication appropriately. Which statement is false?

A) Oral iron preparations must be taken on an empty stomach.

B) When patients are first initiated on iron tablets, they may experience some sort of constipation or diarrhoea, these common side effects are usually transient.

C) The patient must stop taking the medication if they have pink coloured urine.

D) Should the patient experience loss of appetite, then this would require them to see a healthcare professional.

E) If the patient vomits blood, then they must admit themselves to the accident and emergency department.

63. Iron intoxication is a result of overdosing on iron. Systemic toxicity usually occurs when an individual has ingested more than 60mg of elemental iron per kilogram of body mass. Toxicity of iron on the gastrointestinal mucosa can present up to 6 hours post-ingestion. Which of following symptoms is not associated with iron intoxication?

A) Abdominal pain

B) Hypoglycaemia

C) Hematemesis

D) Hypotension

E) Diarrhoea

In the outpatient's clinic, you are about to see Miss RQ, a 54-year-old female who has recently been diagnosed with Type-2 Diabetes. Before you see to her, you are reviewing her PMR. Miss RQ has a family history of Diabetes, with both mother and paternal uncle suffering from the condition. Miss RQ was asymptomatic on initial presentation, with no signs of recent weight loss, thirst, polyuria, or infections. She was referred to her GP for a medical examination following the discovery of glycosuria from urinalysis. Her BMI was 32.2 kg/m^2: above the level of 30kg/m^2. In addition, the patient's waist circumference is 129cm; above the obesity threshold of 102cm. Last fasting blood glucose was 12.2mmol/mol. HbA1c above the diagnostic threshold level. Blood pressure and triglycerides were elevated, while HDL was moderately decreased. Thus, the patient was at high risk from the metabolic syndrome. Otherwise, Miss RA is in overall good health and has no other co-morbidities and is one no other medication.

64. You call Miss RQ, into the consultation room to discuss her most recent blood, urine test results. She explains that recently her thirst and frequency of urination has increased drastically. Upon assessing her urine test results, you find that there was trace of protein in the urine while Miss RQ was receiving no medication. Which one of the following statements best describe the aetiology of what Miss RQ is experiencing?

    A. **Proteinuria is a sensitive marker for progressive renal dysfunction.**

    B. **Proteinuria is associated with a higher eGFR rate.**

    C. **Proteinuria is independent of the glomerular filtration rate.**

    D. **Proteinuria is a sensitive marker for a progressive decline of hepatocyte function.**

    E. **Proteinuria is not a profound symptom of diabetes mellitus.**

65. Miss RQ asks you for the aims of managing Diabetes. You discuss the advantages for her to reduce her body weight, increase physical activity and the importance of having a healthier diet for an overall improvement and in her glycaemic control. What could Miss RQ do to help with achieving this?

A) Increase her alcohol intake to up to 14 units per week.

B) Increase intake of saturated fatty foods

C) Starting weight-loss target should be to lose 5% to 10% of your weight.

D) Tell the patient to decrease dietary calorie intake, to fast intermittently.

E) Encourage the patient to consume 'diabetic friendly' snacks and foods only.

66. Miss RQ often has long commutes to her place of work. She works for a locum agency that requires her to drive daily to work. She is worried that her newly diagnosed condition may hinder her from driving. You provide an answer to her concerns. Which of the following statements best addresses her concerns?

A) Miss RQ can drive, however if her blood-glucose is 3.9mmol/litre, she should not drive. However, if she is already driving, then she must stop the car and remove herself from the driver's seat.

B) Blood-glucose should always be above 4mmol/litre while driving.

C) Miss RQ can drive, however if her blood-glucose is 5.9mmol/litre, she should not drive. However, if she is already driving, then she must stop the car and remove herself from the driver's seat.

D) Miss RQ does not need to carry any glucose snacks.

E) Miss RQ does need to notify the DVLA of her most recent hypoglycaemic episode.

67. You receive a call at your community pharmacy from a representative of a patient asking to speak with the pharmacist. They explain that they have been on a long drive up north, and that the patient who is diabetic has become rather pale, verbally incoherent, and shaky with excessive sweating. The patient is currently driving and the representative on the phone is worried and would like your advice. What is the patient most likely experiencing?

A) Hypertension

B) Hypoglycaemia

C) Hyperglycaemia

D) Hypercholesterolaemia

E) Hyperkalaemia

68. Now that you have determined that the patient has hypoglycaemia. What advice would you give to a patient who is driving that has sub-therapeutic plasma glucose levels of below 4 mmol/litre?

A) The patient must park the vehicle in a safe place and remove themselves from the driver's seat. To consume a glucose food or drink and wait at least 45 minutes after plasma glucose levels have returned to therapeutic levels above 5 mmol/litre.

B) The patient must park the vehicle in a safe place and remain in the driver's seat. To consume a glucose food or drink and wait at least 45 minutes after plasma glucose levels have returned to therapeutic levels above 5 mmol/litre.

C) The patient must park the vehicle in a safe place and remain in the driver's seat. To consume a glucose food or drink and wait at least 30 minutes after plasma glucose levels have returned to therapeutic levels above 5☐mmol/litre.

D) The patient must park the vehicle in a safe place and remain in the driver's seat. To consume a glucose food or drink and wait at least 30 minutes after plasma glucose levels have returned to therapeutic levels above 4mmol/litre.

E) The patient must park the vehicle in a safe place and remain in the driver's seat. To consume a glucose food or drink and wait at least 45 minutes after plasma glucose levels have returned to therapeutic levels above 4mmol/litre.

69. Your trainee pharmacist trainee is shadowing your diabetes clinic today. Mr AX, a 37-year-old male who has been a Type-2 Diabetic has come in for an oral glucose tolerance test to help review his diabetic control. Describe what an oral glucose tolerance test involves?

A) The test involves measuring the plasma-glucose concentration at fasting state, and then to take another measurement 2 hours after at fed state, after consuming a meal.

B) The test involves measuring the plasma-glucose concentration at fasting state, and then to take another measurement 2 hours after at fed state, by drinking a standard anhydrous mannitol solution.

C) The test involves measuring the plasma-glucose concentration at fasting state, and then to take another measurement 20 minutes after at fed state, by drinking a standard anhydrous sorbitol solution.

D) The test involves measuring the plasma-glucose concentration at fasting state, and then to take another measurement 2 hours after at fed state, by drinking a standard anhydrous sorbitol solution.

E) The test involves measuring the plasma-glucose concentration at fasting state, and then to take another measurement 2 hours after at fed state, by drinking a standard anhydrous glucose drink.

70. You are reviewing Mr AX's medications, below is a list of his current medications.
- Metformin 500mg tablet TDS
- Sitagliptin 100mg tablet OD
- Bisoprolol 1.25mg tablet OM
- Senna 7.5mg tablet PRN
- Paracetamol 500mg tablets PRN
- Cholecalciferol 800unit tablet OD

You are discussing Mr AX's recent test results with him. You inform him that he must aim to have a target HbA1C to maintain good diabetic glycaemic control. What should his target HbA1c be?

A) 43 mmol/mol

B) 45 mmol/mol

C) 48 mmol/mol

D) 53 mmol/mol

E) 58 mmol/mol

71. Mrs JB is an 89-year-old female patient who has been a Type-2 diabetic for several years. She has managed her diabetic control with diet and lifestyle measure up until early last year, when she was

initiated on single anti diabetic therapy of Metformin 500mg tablets, to take one tablet BD. Mrs JB also has mild renal impairment and stage one hypertension for which she takes Ramipril 2.5mg capsule OM. Today was her diabetic review and you find that her diabetic control has worsened and requires intensification of anti-diabetic therapy to help manage her diabetes better. You decide to add a second anti-diabetic, a Sulfonylurea. Which one of the following would be best suited for Mrs JB?

A) Glimepiride

B) Gliclazide

C) Alogliptin

D) Glipizide

E) Pioglitazone

72. Miss BM is a newly diagnosed Type-2 diabetic patient who was initiated on a titrating dose of Metformin 500mg tablets. She tells you that she has had continuous diarrhoea, stomach pains and feeling of nausea since starting the new medication. She would like advice as to what she should not do?

A) The patient is most probably experiencing severe gastrointestinal side effects from the Metformin. She can stop taking the metformin as she is not tolerating it well and seek to take an alternative such as a Sulfonylurea.

B) The patient is most probably experiencing severe gastrointestinal side effects from the Metformin. She can stop taking the Metformin as she is not tolerating it well and seek to take an alternative such as a Dipeptidyl Peptidase-4 inhibitor.

C) The patient is most probably experiencing severe gastrointestinal side effects from the Metformin. She can stop taking the Metformin as she is not tolerating it well and seek to take an alternative such as a Pioglitazone.

D) The patient is most probably experiencing gastrointestinal side effects from the Metformin. She could ask to get a prolonged release preparation to be prescribed instead of the standard release Metformin.

E) The patient must continue to take her Metformin as instructed.

73. Today you are reviewing Mr AD's medication during a reconciliation session. His doctor has advised to try an alternative anti diabetic agent for him as his current medications have proven to be insufficient in controlling his diabetes, as portrayed by his most recent blood test results. Mr AD will be initiated on a Glucagon-Like Peptide-1 (GLP-1) receptor agonist and taken off the Sulfonylurea that he is already taking. Which of the following would be an example of the new medication that MR AD would start taking?

A) Vildagliptin

B) Lixisenatide

C) Glimepiride

D) Tolbutamide

E) Repaglinide

74. A newly diagnosed Type-1 diabetic has come into the pharmacy asking to speak with yourself, the pharmacist. They are a bit confused with their insulin regimen and are worried that they may take the incorrect dose. They have contacted their GP for advice but are still awaiting a call back from the doctor. Hence, they came to speak with the pharmacist. You ask the patient to explain what they have understood about their medication. The patient tells you, that they think that insulin Degludec must be taken with every main meal, so to be injected three times daily. The patient also explains that the insulin Aspart must be injected once daily. How would you respond?

A) The patient has correctly described how they must use their insulin. Therefore, to take no action.

B) The patient must be informed that the insulin Aspart is an intermediate acting insulin. So, must be injected between mealtimes.

C) The patient must be informed that the insulin Aspart is a rapid acting insulin, so must be injected at mealtimes with food. The insulin Degludec is a long-acting insulin. So, must be injected once daily to maintain the patient's basal insulin levels, not to be injected with every meal.

D) The patient must be informed that the insulin Aspart is a rapid acting insulin, so must be injected at mealtimes with food. The insulin Degludec is a soluble insulin. So, must be injected once or twice daily to maintain the patient's basal insulin levels, not to be injected with every meal.

E) The patient must be informed that the insulin Degludec is a short acting insulin. So, must be injected after meals.

75. Which of the following statements about diabetic Ketoacidosis is false?
    A) **To monitor blood-ketone and blood-glucose concentrations hourly and adjust the insulin infusion rate accordingly.**
    B) **To ensure that the blood pH is above 7.3 and the patient can eat and drink.**
    C) **Diabetic ketoacidosis is defined as the deficiency of insulin in the body.**
    D) **Once blood-glucose concentration falls below 14□mmol/Litre, glucose 10% should be given by intravenous infusion.**
    E) **The management of diabetic ketoacidosis involves the replacement of fluid and electrolytes and the administration of salbutamol.**

76. Mr XC is a 41-year-old male, he has recently been diagnosed with moderate acute asthma. Which of the following diagnostic parameters would categorise Mr XC's asthma as moderate?
    A) **Peak flow >□50-75%**
    B) **Peak flow >□75-90%**
    C) **Peak flow >□90-100%**
    D) **Peak flow >□35-50%**
    E) **Peak flow >□20-35%**

77. On the acute unit, a patient has been admitted with symptoms of breathlessness, extreme tiredness, and severe headache. The patient's heart rate

>□88 beats/minute, arterial oxygen saturation (SpO2) was 90%. Which one of the following could the patient be diagnosed with?

A) **Moderate acute asthma**

B) **Severe acute asthma**

C) **Bronchitis**

D) **Emphysema**

E) **Life threatening asthma**

78. Mr RW is a 52-year-old recreational athlete with a medical history that is rather significant for asthma, for which he has been using an Albuterol rescue inhaler approximately four times per week, over the past 6 months. During this time, the patient complained that he has also been waking up at night from his sleep with worsening of asthma symptoms approximately three times a month. This has led to several unscheduled asthma visits for symptomatic flares. Today you are seeing Mr RW as he has been diagnosed with life threatening asthma. Which one of the following is not an associated symptom?

A) **Cyanosis**

B) **Arrhythmia**

C) **Exhaustion**

D) **Hypertension**

E) **Unconscious**

79. Mr AC is a 54-year-old male who has been diagnosed with acute coronary syndrome. His most recent ECG has shown that he presents with consistent abnormal QRS waves. Mr AC has also had a blood test; his cardiac bio markers suggest that there are low-level elevations of cardiac troponin-T. The consultant had requested to get an

urgent chest X-Ray and angiography to assess the patient's current situation. Which of the following would suggest that Mr AC has suffered from an ST-Segment Elevation Myocardial Infarction?

A) **Unstable angina**

B) **Partial occlusion of a peripheral vein**

C) **Occlusion of the coronary artery**

D) **Hypertension**

E) **Pulmonary oedema**

80. Managing a patient with acute coronary syndrome can involve pharmacological and non-pharmacological interventions. What would be the primary aim for the management of a STEMI?

A) **Restore coronary arterial blood flow**

B) **Restore glomerular blood flow**

C) **Restore hepatocellular blood flow**

D) **Increase arterial blood pressure**

E) **Reduce levels of protein cardiac biomarkers such as troponin T**

81. Any patient experiencing a myocardial infarction should receive immediate treatment. An anti-platelet such as Aspirin should be administered to prevent platelet congregation. Opioids along with Glyceryl-Trinitrate can be administered to the patient also as a relieving pain relief treatment. Which of the following monitoring requirements are necessary for the patient when management an MI?

A) **All patients admitted to hospital should be closely monitored for hyperkalaemia.**

B) **All patients admitted to hospital should be closely monitored for hyperglycaemia.**

C) All patients admitted to hospital should be closely monitored for hypernatremia.

D) All patients admitted to hospital should be closely monitored for hypercalcaemia.

E) All patients admitted to hospital should be closely monitored for hypercholesterolemia.

82. The cardiology team has successfully managed Mr AC's condition and following the ACS, you have offered a cardiac rehabilitation programme to him which includes advice for lifestyle changes. Which of the following advice statement would you tell Mr AC?

A) Mr AC must moderate his dietary fat intake to ensure he has a high LDL to HDL ratio.

B) Mr AC must lose body weight to maintain a healthy BMI under 18kg/m^2.

C) Mr AC must stop smoking, you may refer him to your local smoking cessation service.

D) Mr AC may regularly drink up to 21 units of alcohol per week.

E) Mr AC should skip meals frequently to maintain a balanced diet.

83. Prior to Mr AC's hospital discharge, you are carrying out medicines' reconciliation for his current medication to optimize drug usage. His current medication includes the following:

- Lisinopril tablet 20mg OD
- Atorvastatin tablet 10mg OD
- Omeprazole gastro resistant capsule 20mg OM
- Cholecalciferol 800 unit capsule OD
- Warfarin tablets ASD

Which of the following medication would be prescribed for the patient?

A) **Aspirin must be prescribed for the patient for 12 months post myocardial infarction as an antiplatelet.**

B) **Dual antiplatelet therapy with an anticoagulant must be avoided with Mr AC.**

C) **Aspirin can be used with a second antiplatelet, such as Clopidogrel. This second antiplatelet should be continued for up to 12 months unless contraindicated.**

D) **Unfractionated Heparin must be continued indefinitely.**

E) **Diltiazem is indicated for those patients who have pulmonary congestion.**

84. Miss KP is a 78-year-old female who has been admitted into the medical unit. She has had presented with a raised heart rate which she describes as racing. She has been feeling rather breathless and has a body temperature of 35.6°C with darkened coloured lips. Her medical history shows that she has been on a chronic treatment regimen of Prednisolone 30mg daily to manage her Crohn's since the last 14 months. The records also state that the patient has an acute history of recreational drug abuse. Her arms have several cuts, grazes, and bruises. She is conscious but

rather confused. Which of the following could the patient have?

A) **Cytokine storm**

B) **Hyperthyroid attack**

C) **Diabetic ketoacidosis**

D) **Sepsis**

E) **Community acquired pneumonia**

85. You are going through clinical responding to symptoms training with your pharmacy technician. Which of the following is not a sign of sepsis?

A) **Not passed urine in previous 8 hours**

B) **Respiratory rate of 25 breaths per minute or above**

C) **Systolic blood pressure 90 mmHg or less**

D) **Non-blanching rash of skin**

E) **Altered mental state**

86. You are now producing training material for your dispensary team at your community pharmacy to train your staff on recognising symptoms of sepsis and how to differentiate between diagnosis of adults and child. Which of the following would be classed as a high-risk factor for contracting sepsis in a child aged between 5-11 years?

A) **Pyrexia**

B) **Raised heart rate**

C) **Dry skin**

D) **Pupil dilation**

E) **Hyperactive child**

87. You are assessing a drug chart for a patient who is currently on several medications. He has now been prescribed intravenous antibiotics to manage his septic shock. Which of the following current medications would be classed as placing the patient in a high-risk category for contracting sepsis?

   A) Methotrexate 2.5mg tablets

   B) Omeprazole 20 tablets

   C) Topical 0.1% paraffin ointment

   D) Folic acid 5mg tablets

   E) Amlodipine 5mg tablets

88. On the geriatric ward, a patient is presenting with a typical UTI. Her symptoms include needing to pee suddenly, burning sensation when peeing with pain in your lower tummy and the patient was rather confused. She has no other allergies and is on no other medications. Which of the following medications would be recommended as an oral first-line treatment for this patient?

   A) Metronidazole

   B) Nitrofurantoin

   C) Trimethoprim

   D) Gentamicin

   E) Co-Amoxiclav

89. A prescription is handed in to you to be dispensed as soon as possible as it is for an urgent antibiotic. The patient is a care home patient who is suffering from a lower UTI. On the patients PMR there is a note stating that the patient has acute intrinsic renal failure with a history of gall bladder inflammation which is being investigated. You determine that the Nitrofurantoin prescribed is not suitable for this

patient as his estimated glomerular filtration rate (eGFR) contraindicates the drug for him. Which of the following eGFR reading would cause this?

A) 28 ml/min/1.73 m^2

B) 40 ml/min/1.73 m^2

C) 46 ml/min/1.73 m^2

D) 55 ml/min/1.73 m^2

E) 75 ml/min/1.73 m^2

90. A patient with glucose metabolism impairment has a routine urine test at his phlebotomy clinic today. He already had been taking a short course of Nitrofurantoin for a recent urinary tract infection which has now subsided. Last night was his last dose. Why should the urine test be rescheduled?

A) **False negative urinary glucose test result**

B) **False positive urinary calcium test result**

C) **False positive urinary glucose test result**

D) **False negative urinary sodium test result**

E) **False positive urinary haemoglobin test result**

91. You are the senior rotational pharmacist who is seeing to a patient who has been admitted with pneumonia. Your trust guidelines state that any adult admitted with community-acquired pneumonia (CAP) in hospital must have a mortality risk assessment carried out using the CURB65 score. What does the acronym stand for?

A) **Confusion, Urea nitrogen level raised over 7 mmol/litre in the blood,**

Respiratory rate (of 30 breaths per minute or more per minute), Blood pressure lower than 60 mmHg (diastolic) / 90 mmHg (systolic), Age 65 years or less.

B) Confusion, Urea nitrogen level raised over 7 mmol/litre in the blood, Respiratory rate (of 28 breaths per minute or less per minute), Blood pressure lower than 60 mmHg (diastolic) / 90 mmHg (systolic), Age 65 years or more.

C) Confusion, Urea nitrogen level raised over 5 mmol/litre in the blood, Respiratory rate (of 30 breaths per minute or more per minute), Blood pressure lower than 60 mmHg (diastolic) / 90 mmHg (systolic), Age 65 years or more.

D) Confusion, Urea nitrogen level raised over 7 mmol/litre in the blood, Respiratory rate (of 30 breaths per minute or more per minute), Blood pressure lower than 80 mmHg (diastolic) / 120 mmHg (systolic), Age 65 years or more.

E) Confusion, Urea nitrogen level raised over 7 mmol/litre in the blood, Respiratory rate (of 30 breaths per minute or more per minute), Blood pressure lower than 60 mmHg (diastolic) / 90 mmHg (systolic), Age 65 years or more.

92. When interpreting a CURB65 score calculated from a patient. What score would place the patient at a high risk of mortality?

    A) 0

    B) 1

    C) 2

    D) 5

    E) 6

93. After clinically assessing a patient with community acquired pneumonia. Your multidisciplinary team determine that the patient has a low mortality risk as his CURB65 score was 1. The patient has nothing stated in his allergy status on his drug chart, which of the following antibiotic would be prescribed as a first-line treatment?

    A) Metronidazole 200mg

    B) Amoxicillin 500mg

    C) Clarithromycin 250mg

    D) Co-Amoxiclav 125mg/500 mg

    E) Erythromycin 500mg

94. Today you are very busy in the dispensary. A patient approaches the counter asking to purchase a decongestant for herself. She explains that she thinks she has a sinus related headache with a blocked nose. She has also developed a sore throat and bruising on her arm. She asks to purchase something to help with her symptoms. You question her further and she tells you that she recently did start a medication that begins with a letter 'C' for her high thyroid. How would you respond?

A) Sell the patient an OTC preparation containing ephedrine.

B) Refuse to make the sale and refer, the patient is presumably talking about Carbamazepine, and has experienced adverse effects.

C) Sell the patient an OTC preparation containing Pseudoephedrine.

D) Refuse to make the sale and refer, the patient is presumably talking about Carbimazole, and has experienced adverse effects.

E) Sell the patient a topical nasal spray to manage her symptoms acutely.

Mr GY is a 37-year-old male patient, who presents with a three week complaint of retrosternal heart burn that is aggravated with lying down flat after a meal. Mr GY also informs you that the discomfort lasts for about three to four hours, if it occurs at night then it prevents him from sleeping. He also tells you that he has tried using OTC antacids from his local supermarket which only offer short-term relief.

Medical History
- No Known Allergies
- Stage 1 Hypertension for three years
- Generalised Anxiety Disorder (managed by cognitive behavioural therapy)

Social History
Mr GY is a single parent with a young daughter. He drinks 4 units of alcohol daily since he was a teenager and smokes 15 cigarettes per day.

Current medications
- Amlodipine 5mg OD
- Loratadine 10mg OD PRN
- Paracetamol 500mg PRN
- Multivitamin supplement OD

95. Mr GY has been referred to the pharmacy team to seek some advice about managing his state with diet and lifestyle measures. Which of the following would not be advised to the patient?

A) Smoking cessation

B) Eating food in smaller portions

C) Eating food at least an hour before bed

D) To raise the bed at the head level

E) Moderate exercise

96. Your trainee pharmacist is shadowing your consultation with Mr GY. You advice the patient that his current state may develop into Gastroesophageal Reflux Disease. The trainee asks you more about this. How would you respond?

A) After ingestion, the contents in the stomach can escape from the sphincter into the oesophageal cavity. This causes symptoms of heartburn, nausea, and regurgitation, and potential inflammation.

B) The contents in the stomach can escape from the sphincter into the intestinal cavity. This causes symptoms of abdominal distention, and potential inflammation.

C) After ingestion, the contents in the stomach can cause cramping. Along with the cramps, you get greasy, green coloured vomiting.

D) The contents in the stomach can escape from the sphincter into the intestinal cavity. This can promote abdominal pain and blood-stained stools.

E) After ingestion, the contents in the stomach can escape from the sphincter into the oesophageal cavity. This causes symptoms of dysphagia, weight loss and chest pain.

97. Mrs SV, a 72-year-old female teacher presented with three months' history of dyspepsia. More recently she had developed epigastric pain. This was accompanied with unintentional weight loss of five kilograms. Otherwise, she is in good health with no history of nausea, vomiting, abdominal distension, haematemesis, diarrhoea, constipation, night sweats, or fevers. Her medical notes suggest no history of morbidities. The only medication was Lansoprazole. She drank no alcohol and smoked 50 cigarettes/day. Examination was unremarkable. All blood tests, including full blood count, biochemistry, and lactate dehydrogenase, were normal. What OTC medication would you recommend if necessary?

A) Sell the patient a Sodium Alginate/Sodium Bicarbonate heart burn relief solution.

B) Do not make a sale and refer the patient to the local smoking cessation service.

C) Sell the patient an Aluminium hydroxide/Simethicone symptom relieving agent.

D) Sell the patient a Bismuth-containing antacids.

E) Refer the patient for an urgent investigation, do not make any sale.

98. A 49-year-old man was referred to your department for a 1-year history of dyspepsia responsive to oral proton pump-inhibitor therapy. During the last year, he underwent a gastroscopy and a computed tomography according to the instructions of the consultant that failed to reveal an underlying organic disease. This patient has been complaining of having an ache or burning pain in the abdomen, pain that is worse when his stomach is empty. The consultant refuses to diagnose the patient with functional dyspepsia and has requested him to undertake another diagnostic test. Which of the following test would the patient have been requested for?

A) Endoscopy

B) Urea 13C breath test for H.Pylori infection

C) Physical abdominal examination for distention

D) Full Blood count blood test for gastroenteritis

E) Oral glucose tolerance test

99. A patient has informed you that she has an endoscopy procedure at the end of this month. He has brought in his pre-assessment letter for you to interpret as he is very confused. The letter states that if the patient is taking any medications such as PPI's, then they must stop this at least 14 days before the endoscopy. Which of the following statement explains why this may be?

A) Cimetidine can mask symptoms of oesophageal cancer

B) Calcium carbonate can cause erosion of the parietal layer

C) Bismuth subsalicylate can promote nausea

D) Omeprazole can mask symptoms of gastric cancer/malignancy

E) Famotidine can mask symptoms of oesophageal cancer

100.   You are carrying out a structured medication review in a general practice with a patient. After going through each medication, the patient informs you that she does not take her weekly Alendronic acid tablets as she is scared. You question her further about this matter. The patient stated that her mother used to take this medication for her bones and ended up dying because of oesophageal cancer. Her worry of ending up in a similar situation affects her adherence. You acknowledge her concerns and explain the benefits of slowing bone degeneration with the medication. How should you counsel her?

A) She must take with plenty of water while upright, on an empty stomach. She must remain upright for at least 30 minutes after administration.

B) Folic acid supplementation must commence prior to starting Bisphosphonates.

C) Oesophageal strictures are a common side effect.

D) She must take with plenty of water while upright, on an empty stomach. She must remain upright for at least 15 minutes after administration.

E) She can take Alendronic acid with her main meal.

101.   You are overseeing the training of nursing students after a seminar at your hospital trust. They are discussing a case study in which the patient has experienced heart failure with reduced ejection fraction. Which of the following statement best describes this?

A) **Heart failure associated with reduced ejection fraction, presents with an ejection fraction of less than 20%.**

B) **Heart failure associated with reduced ejection fraction, is caused by the right ventricle losing the ability to contract optimally and therefore presents with an ejection fraction of less than 40%.**

C) **Heart failure associated with reduced ejection fraction, presents with an increase in the stroke volume.**

D) **Heart failure associated with reduced ejection fraction, is caused by the left ventricle not contracting optimally and therefore, presents with an ejection fraction of less than 40%.**

E) **Heart failure associated with reduced ejection fraction, the left atria lose its ability to contract normally and therefore presents with an ejection fraction of less than 50%.**

102. Your trainees are now discussing the potential treatments a patient with heart failure associated with reduced ejection fraction could have. Which of the following would be suitable therapeutically for such a patient?

A) **Ramipril with Bisoprolol**

B) **Verapamil Hydrochloride**

C) **Nifedipine with Digoxin**

D) **Diltiazem with Bisoprolol**

E) **Nicardipine with Lisinopril**

103. Patient AV is a 49-year-old male who has a family history of chronic heart failure. He has been told by the doctor that he is at substantial risk of developing it also according to his most recent ECG results. Today he has come into you to seek advice as to how he could improve his health through diet and lifestyle measures. Which of the following statement would be false?

A) **If the patient is a smoker, then to stop smoking**

B) **The patient should reduce alcohol consumption to no more than 14 units per week**

C) **He should eat no more than 6g of salt a day (2.4g sodium)**

D) **The patient should be advised to reduce saturated fat intake**

E) **Salt substitutes containing potassium should be considered as an alternative**

104. GL is a 45-year-old female who has successfully managed her chronic heart failure with medication that she tolerates well. However, the doctor who reviewed her today has identified that she now presents with stable angina also, thus,

would like to alter her medications. Which of the following single agents could be used to treat both conditions?

A) Nifedipine

B) Diphenhydramine

C) Amlodipine

D) Atropine

E) Nicardipine

105. You are a clinical pharmacist carrying out ward rounds, today you are seeing to Mr HT, a 67 year old male who has developed very swollen lower limbs. He cannot walk and now has become immobile. His past medical history states that he has chronic heart failure, hypertension and has also suffered from a TIA about 13 years ago. The patient also states of experiencing breathlessness at rest and lately feeling rather tired all the time. Which of the following is most likely a probable diagnosis for Mr HT?

A) Worsening of glycaemic control, causing fatigue.

B) Worsening of heart failure, causing congestive symptoms.

C) The patient has most probably experienced another cardiovascular event such as a TIA, requires urgent medical attention.

D) The patient is experiencing a deep vein thrombosis.

E) These are symptoms of severe hypertension, requires immediate medical assistance.

106. The ward rounds are now complete, and the multidisciplinary team is reviewing Mr HT's medical notes and observations from the round. The team determine to start him on a short course of a medication to help with his symptoms of peripheral oedema. Which of the following would be best for Mr HT?

A) Furosemide 20mg OD

B) Bendroflumethiazide 2.5mg OD

C) Digoxin 125mcg

D) Warfarin 5mg OD

E) Spironolactone 25mg OD

107. You are asked about extrapyramidal symptoms and what they may be. Which of the below is not an extrapyramidal symptom?

A) Akathisia

B) Tardive dyskinesia

C) Coughing

D) Dystonia,

E) Involuntary movements

108. The NHS contractually requires a pharmacy that provides NHS services to offer 'essential services' as a minimum? Which of the following is not an essential service?

A) New medicines service

B) Dispensing medications

C) Clinical governance

D) Discharge medicines service

E) Disposal of unwanted medications

109. Your trainee pharmacist is revising about high-risk medications. You point out that Hydroxychloroquine is also one. Any patient who takes this agent must be monitored for ocular toxicity. Which of the following symptoms are not associated with such toxicity?

A) Ocular discharge

B) Decreased vision

C) Flashing lights

D) Glare

E) Ocular pain

110. In the recent clinic letter for patient X, the consultant advised to prescribe a Dipeptidyl Peptidase-4 inhibitor for the patient to better manage his Type-2 diabetes. The patient already takes Quinine 200mg ON for nocturnal cramps, Warfarin ASD and Paracetamol PRN. She currently has an eGFR of 37mL/minute/1.73 m^2. Which of the following drugs would be best to prescribe for patient X?

A) Empagliflozin

B) Sitagliptin

C) Rosuvastatin

D) Linagliptin

E) Liraglutide

111. The duty doctor today has handed over a patient to you. A 76-year-old diabetic male who has had a foot ulcer and has hospital-acquired septicaemia. The patient has been prescribed an IV ABX dose of 500mg BD. The formulary states that the standard dose for this indication is 23mg/kg every 8–12□hours. The patient is 181cm tall, and weighs 67kg, his recent blood tests found that his

serum WBC count was 4.0 - 11.0 x 10*9/L, the serum creatinine level was 220 µmol/L. You are now screening his medication requests. Which of the following would be most appropriate?

You can use the following information:
Use ABX with caution in patients with sensitivity to beta-lactam antibacterial. Use half normal dose every 12 hours if creatinine clearance 10–25 mL/minute. Manufacturer advises monitor liver function due to risk of hepatotoxicity.

A) Advice the doctor to prescribe IV 500mg of ABX every 12 hours

B) Advice the doctor to prescribe IV 750mg of ABX every 12 hours

C) Advice the doctor to prescribe IV 1000mg of ABX every 12 hours

D) Advice the doctor to prescribe IV 1500mg of ABX every 12 hours

E) Advice the doctor to prescribe IV 2000mg of ABX every 8 hours

112.   What are the benefits of using Carbocisteine for the patient?

A) Increases urine output

B) Lowers MCV

C) Increases exogenous function

D) Reduces sputum viscosity

E) Increase dermal vasodilation

113. According to NICE guidelines, which blood test should be measured in a 75-year-old starting on Atorvastatin?

A) Urea

B) Alanine aminotransferase

C) Creatinine

D) Erythrocyte sedimentation rate

E) Glomerular filtration rate

114. Your dispenser is going to process a walk-in prescription that has been handed by a patient. She notices that on the prescription it states 'SLS' next to one of the items, she asks what this means?

A) SLS stands for selected list scheme, this is a list of medications/products which is listed by the drug tariff that prescribers may only prescribe under certain conditions.

B) SLS stands for selected licensing scheme. This scheme states that only specialist prescribers with postgraduate qualifications can prescribe schedule 1 controlled drugs.

C) SLS stands for selected licensing scheme. This scheme states that only specialist prescribers who are registered with the home office can prescribe schedule 1 controlled drugs.

D) SLS stands for social liability scheme. This scheme states that minors under the age of 16 cannot purchase OTC

medications that are licensed as 'pharmacy only'.

E) SLS stands for selected list scheme, this is a list of medications/products which is listed by the local CCG that are blacklisted for prescribers to prescribe on an FP10SS form.

115. You are asking Mrs QW her medication history. She tells you that she is taking Omeprazole capsules in the morning to protect her stomach. She also takes Oxybutynin as pain relief for her back and Sodium Alginate PRN for dyspepsia. She has recently finished a course of Carbimazole for her overactive thyroid which is now under control. What may be incorrect from her medication history?

A) Carbimazole is licensed for hypothyroidism

B) Oxybutynin is an anticholinergic that licensed for an overactive bladder

C) Omeprazole should not be taken alongside a sodium alginate solution

D) Oxybutynin is contraindicated in hyperthyroidism

E) Carbimazole should not be taken at the same time as other medications.

116. A 19-year-old female has a Levonorgestrel 1.5mg tablet prescribed for herself by the GP on an FP10SS form. She has usually never paid for a prescription charge and asks if she still must pay as she is a university student?

A) Zero charge

B) One charge

C) Two charges

D) Age exempt

E) Medical exempt

117. Miss CP, a 32-year-old female was managing her anxiety on Citalopram 20 mg tablets OD very well over the last 4 years. Since the COVID-19 lockdown she has been working from home, recently she has had to go back to the office and has been experiencing anxiety attacks due to the social environment. She has now had her dose of Citalopram increased to 30mg OD. The prescription asks you to dispense 28 days' worth of Citalopram 20mg and 10mg tablets to make up the daily dose. How many prescription charges would you charge her?

A) Zero

B) One

C) Two

D) Three

E) Mental health medications are exempt

118. Drug X is an antibiotic which is dispensed as powder for injection in vials which needs to be reconstituted before being made up. You receive an NHS prescription for a 45-year-old male, it is for 10x drug X vials and 10x 250ml water for injection vials, on one prescription form. How many charges should you take for this prescription?

A) Zero charges

B) One Charge

C) Two charges

D) Four charges

E) 20 charges

119.   You are working as a locum pharmacist today and the dispensary staff has asked to carry out a count on the controlled drugs cabinet to ensure the weekly balance is accurate and up to date. You stumble across an entry for Pizotifen. What schedule-controlled drug is Pizotifen?

   A) Schedule 1

   B) Schedule 2

   C) Schedule 3

   D) Schedule 4

   E) Not a controlled drug

120.   A 17-year-old called the '111' out of hours NHS urgent care service for help. He has a fungal infection on both his thumb nail beds, which is now really bothering him. He has no pain, but the discolouration has worsened. He is concerned about the health of his nails, the out of hour's service has referred him to community pharmacy to purchase an anti-fungal treatment and to seek advice. The patient has no other co-morbidities and is not on any medication. You only have Amorolfine 5% solution available. Can you sell this as a 'P' Pharmacy Only medication?

   A) You cannot make the sale as Amorolfine 5% solution is a POM.

   B) You can make the sale to this patient as Amorolfine 5% solution is a P medication.

   C) You cannot make the sale as Amorolfine 5% solution should not be sold to anyone under the age of 18 years.

   D) You can make the sale to this patient as Amorolfine 5% solution, as it was

recommended by a medical professional.

E) **You cannot make the sale as Amorolfine 5% solution, as it is not indicated for fungal nail infection treatment.**

121.　Mr SS has called your pharmacy to request his repeat medication over the phone. He tells you that he would like to reorder his cream which he uses for his skin carcinoma on his nose. You are unsure as to which cream; he is referring to as he is on several medication. Which of the medications below is Mr SS referring to?

A) **Estriol 0.01% cream**

B) **Piroxicam 0.5% gel**

C) **Betamethasone 0.1% cream**

D) **Mometasone 0.1% ointment**

E) **Fluorouracil 5% cream**

122.　Which of the following drug is indicated to use in drug induced extrapyramidal symptoms?

A) **Primidone**

B) **Carbamazepine**

C) **Dutasteride**

D) **Trihexyphenidyl**

E) **Propranolol**

You are leading a genitourinary session with trainee pharmacists at the local trusts discussing different terms and their relevance to pharmacological drugs. Questions 123-129 below all relate to the following answer option:

A) **Urinary urgency**

B) **The number of times you need to urinate within a period**

C) **Lack voluntary control over urination / defecation**

D) **Bladder instability**

E) **Passing of urine filtrate through the urethra**

F) **Discharge of semen from the reproductive tract**

G) **Process of discharging lining of the uterus**

H) **Benign prostatic hyperplasia**

123.   Mr AY, a 68-year-old male has been experiencing problems with urination. He explains that he in unhappy every time he urinates as he feels that he cannot completely urinate. The doctor has now prescribed Oxybutynin tablets. It is a new medication for him. What is Mr AY experiencing from?

124.   A lady has approached you over the counter and states that she is fed up with having strong immediate needs to urinate. What could she be experiencing?

125.   Your pharmacy technician asks you, what is meant by the term urinary frequency?

126. Mr CF wants to speak to you in private, he states that incontinence has become an issue for him. He is considering purchasing an OTC aid to assist with this. What is he referring to?

127. A female has bought her baby is who keeps wetting his nappies. What process is causing this?

128. Miss DF has been much stressed lately. She tells you that despite being very young, ever since she has given birth to her first child, she cannot hold her urine for prolonged periods of time. What is she most likely experiencing from?

129. A male patient in his late 50's is concerned about his sexual health. He tells you that he used to have sex with his partner 3 times per week. Recently, he has been experiencing pain upon ejaculation. Sometimes his symptoms may be associated with burning and pressure upon urination. What is he experiencing from?

130. A patient who experiences symptoms of urinary frequency, urgency and incontinence can sometimes all be treated by one medication. Which of the following medications could be used for these indications?
   A) Tapentadol
   B) Tamsulosin
   C) Telmisartan
   D) Tolterodine
   E) Terlipressin

131. Clindamycin is a very well-established agent used to tackle infections. It is available in several formulations for different indications. What action does Clindamycin have within a biological body to exert its effect?

A) Acts to inhibit folate synthesis at initial stages

B) Works by interfering the synthesis of the bacterial cell wall

C) It disrupts the cell membrane of the bacteria

D) The agent alters protein synthesis

E) Inhibits mitochondrial respiration

132. Miss AW, a 41-year-old patient has come in to complain about her prescription medication. She picked up tablets yesterday which were intended to be used as period delay tablets. When she opened her medication packet, she found Nortriptyline tablets. She recognized from the name that these are incorrect and has come back to get them replaced. What would be the best course of action to take?

A) Apologize to the patient and give her the pharmacy manager's details.

B) Find out if the patient has taken any of the incorrect medication, to determine level of harm.

C) Check the signature of who accuracy checked the medication on the label and refer the patient to that colleague as it is not your fault.

D) Report this matter to the GPhC for further investigation.

E) Inform the patient that this medication is correct. It is indicated for her requirement.

133. Miss AW asks about the mode of action of Nortriptyline and what it is used for as she has never heard of this drug before, what do you tell her?

A) Nortriptyline is a selective serotonin inhibitor, that increases the synaptic concentration of serotonin only.

B) Nortriptyline is a selective acetylcholine inhibitor, that increases the synaptic concentration of acetylcholine only.

C) Nortriptyline is a selective dopamine inhibitor, that increases the synaptic concentration of dopamine.

D) Nortriptyline is a selective noradrenaline inhibitor, that increases the synaptic concentration of noradrenaline.

E) Nortriptyline is a selective serotonin and norepinephrine inhibitor, that increases the synaptic concentration of serotonin and norepinephrine.

134. You have now taken back the Nortriptyline that was incorrectly dispensed and dispense the correct drug for her. What drug would have been prescribed originally on the prescription for Miss AW?

A) Norethisterone

B) Naltrexone

C) Nevibolol

D) Nitroglycerin

E) Nateglinide

135. The Renin-Angiotensin-Aldosterone system (RAAS) is a hormone which essentially regulates the bodies fluid level and blood pressure. Which of the following drugs are RAAS acting drugs?
A) Bisoprolol

B) Verapamil

C) Losartan

D) Phentolamine

E) Doxazosin

136. You are a prescribing pharmacist within a general practice. A gentleman has come seeking to get some sort of medication for his erectile dysfunction. You consider prescribing Sildenafil PRN for him. Which of the following would not be a caution for when using Sildenafil?
A) Penile angulation

B) Peyronie's disease

C) Sickle cell anaemia

D) Hypertension

E) Leukaemia

137. Medical students are undergoing their renal workshop today. You are explaining the differences between the glomerular filtration rate (GFR) and creatinine clearance. Which of the following best describes GFR?
A) GFR is the amount of urine passed through the glomeruli per minute.

B) GFR is the amount of urine passed through the glomeruli per hour.

C) GFR is the amount of creatinine passed through the glomeruli per minute.

D) GFR is the amount of blood passed through the glomeruli per minute.

E) GFR is the amount of filtrate passed through the glomeruli per minute.

138. A 64-year-old female patient had an exacerbation of asthma. The patient already has several medications for her cardiovascular co-morbidities. Her new medication administration record chart shows that she has been prescribed (Drug X) for her anxiety. Which of the medications listed below could be cautioned in this patient?

A) Propranolol

B) Sertraline

C) Citalopram

D) Fluoxetine

E) Topiramate

139. Mrs CV is 74-years-old female. She has presented today with worsening chest pain and explains that her breathlessness is worse are night, accompanied with a dry cough which wakes her up. She had tried treating her cough with pholcodine OTC, to help but the symptoms have not subsided. Upon further examination she also informs you that the left, lower calf feels very heavy and painful and that randomly she has pink coloured phlegm being produced. What do you think she is suffering from?

A) Atrial fibrillation

B) Deep vein thrombosis

C) Heart failure

D) Coronary occlusion

E) Peripheral oedema

140. An elderly patient, 74-year-old male patient was admitted with progressive increase in breathlessness, cough, and ankle oedema over the previous 4 weeks. His general practitioner had prescribed oral amoxicillin for a recent chest infection 4 weeks ago, however the symptoms have not subsided. He had suffered from dyspepsia, increasing over recent weeks. Upon admission you note a murmur of the heart which warrants further investigation. After an abnormal ECG, your team determines cause of dyspnoea to be cardiac related. Typical congestive heart failure associated with oedema is usually treated with which of the following agents as first line.

A) Furosemide

B) Verapamil

C) Nicorandil

D) Spironolactone

E) Amlodipine

141. Today you are working as a locum pharmacist in the community. It is a very busy Sunday afternoon and a male in his early 30's approaches you to seek advice about a rash around his right eye. He explains that he returned from the Philippines last Thursday and the rash has got worse and very sore. The rash runs from his eye down to his neck. The patient takes no other medications, otherwise is healthy. You suspect that he may have a form of shingles. What advice do you give him?

A) Sell him Chloramphenicol eye drops to help with his symptoms.

B) Recommend bathing the eye with an antiviral solution.

C) Refer the patient to another pharmacy as you do not stock antiviral eye drops.

D) Refer the patient to seek urgent medical care.

E) Tell the patient to return home as his condition should subside in the next 5-7 days.

142. A patient has been prescribed a new medication which he must take daily as prophylaxis. The nurse has advised to cover up when going outside in the sunshine and not to expose his skin too much to UV sunlight rays. Which of the following drug would this be?

A) Citalopram

B) Doxycycline

C) Omeprazole

D) Clopidogrel

E) Phenoxymethylpenicillin

143. A patient has come in to collect his regular repeat medication, he states that he would like to change this medication to a different one as it has affected his taste buds. His taste is no longer the same and it has affected his eating habits. Which of the following could this be?

A) **Metformin**

B) **Gliclazide**

C) **Warfarin**

D) **Sulfinpyrazone**

E) **Sildenafil**

144. A Patient has come into the pharmacy to report her adverse effects that she has been experiencing since starting her medication. She explains that while taking Microgynon 30®, she feels quite tight in the chest often painful and at night reports of feeling breathless. She has been using the contraceptive for 2 months and is worried that it may be the new medication. What is the most likely cause of this adverse effect?

A. **Lung carcinoma**

B. **Emphysema**

C. **Pulmonary embolism**

D. **Asthma**

E. **Lung abscess**

145. Miss PL, called your pharmacy this morning wanting to speak with you. She is a regular patient of yours and comes into the pharmacy daily for her supervised consumption. She tells you that she has been feeling very tired and often sleepy during the day over the last week. Over the last two mornings she has been waking with a severe headache. You question her further and find that she has been

eating and drinking as normal. Recently she had an FBC, LFT and U&E tested which all were normal. She denies use of any recreational drugs and has been teetotal from alcohol since April last year. You notice her cyanosed lips, she asks to purchase strong caffeine tablets to help with her symptoms.

Below is a list of her medications:

- *Aspirin 75mg tablet OD*
- *Paracetamol 500mg QDS PRN*
- *Methadone 1mg/ml sugar free oral solution 65ml taken daily (SUPERVISED)*
- *Citalopram 20mg Tablet OM*
- *Amlodipine 5mg Tablet OD*
- *Aqueous cream 500g AD PRN*

What could be the reason for her current state?

A) **The patient is experiencing symptoms of alcohol withdrawal, inform the patient that she must speak to her GP as she requires Naltrexone.**

B) **The patient is experiencing symptoms of general tiredness, sell her a stimulant such a caffeine. Also counsel the patient on sleep hygiene as it will help with her quality of sleep.**

C) **Advice the patient to have her Iron and haemoglobin levels checked, she may have a deficiency that needs to be addressed.**

D) **Sell the patient multivitamins and counsel the patient on sleep hygiene as it will help with her quality of sleep.**

E) **The patient is experiencing symptoms of respiratory depression, discuss this with her keyworker/prescriber and tell the patient to seek medical attention.**

146.   A prescription for a 14-month-old baby is bought into your pharmacy to be dispensed. The RX is requesting Chloramphenicol 0.5% eye drops solution for a conjunctival eye infection. You have only one bottle available on your shelf in stock. Which of the following constituents should be avoided in this patient?

A) **Water for injection**

B) **Phenyl nitrate**

C) **Boric acid**

D) **Chloramphenicol**

E) **None of the above**

147.   An 85-year male patient was admitted to the acute unit. His medical notes state that he was dizzy with visual disturbance upon examination. His consciousness has been altered. He has been feeling nauseous, the nurses have mentioned this to the consultant. Below is a list of his medications:

- Clopidogrel 75mg tablet OD
- Paracetamol 500mg QDS PRN
- Warfarin (As per anticoagulation clinic)
- Digoxin 125mcg Tablet OM
- Ramipril 1.25mg Tablet OD
- Lansoprazole 15mg capsule OM

From the options stated below, what is the patient most likely experiencing from?

A) **Hypokalaemia**

B) **Hyperkalaemia**

C) **Hypercalcaemia**

D) **Hypophosphataemia**

E) **Hypernatraemia**

148.   A 23-year-old male customer is travelling to Marbella tomorrow for 9 days. He suffered a knee injury last month and was prescribed Co-Codamol 8/500mg tablets, which he takes as pain relief until his injury heals. Unfortunately, he has now misplaced these tablets and has come asking for an emergency supply. You tell the patient that this strength of medication is available to purchase over the counter, therefore an emergency supply wouldn't be necessary. The patient typically takes one tablet three times daily when needed. What is the maximum quantity that you could supply to this customer?

A) 16

B) 32

C) 64

D) 84

E) 96

149.   The patient reports drowsiness when taking a medication. Which of her medications is the most likely to cause this?

A) Simvastatin

B) Rivaroxaban

C) Sildenafil

D) Allopurinol

E) Chlorphenamine

150.   Mrs DF, a 73-year-old female patient with chronic hypertension. You see her medical history and note that she has had recent peripheral oedema. Her general practitioner had recently prescribed her Furosemide 20mg OD. On examination she has had nausea, extreme tiredness, and myalgia with cramping. What is the most likely because of her symptoms?

A) Hypernatraemia

B) Hyperkalaemia

C) Hypoglycaemia

D) Hyponatraemia

E) Hyperglycaemia

151.   A young male in his early 20's has come seeking some advice for his headaches. He has frequent migraines and is unsure as to what would trigger them. Which of the following is not a trigger for a migraine attack?

A) Bright light

B) Chocolate

C) Public transport

D) Caffeine

E) Skipping meals

152.   Mr WE, a 76-year-old male has been experiencing blurred vision, associated with a dry mouth and interruption with urine flow which is causing him difficulty. He has not tried anything for the symptoms as he is worried it may interact with his current medication. He takes Amlodipine for hypertension, Amitriptyline for peripheral neuralgia, Paracetamol for headaches, Senna for constipation and Ibuprofen OTC PRN. Which of his medication could cause this as an affect?

A) Amlodipine

B) Amitriptyline

C) Paracetamol

D) Senna

E) Ibuprofen

153. You are reviewing Mr GH's medication with him during his annual diabetic check. You notice that his most recent HbA1C reading was sub-therapeutic at 108mmol/mol. The patient currently has a BMI of 42kg/m², is an active smoker but does not drink alcohol. You question his management of his condition, he tells you that he takes the Metformin as prescribed, but has not been taking 'the other' diabetes medication as it makes him urinate far too frequently. As he is a lorry driver he cannot carry on using that medication. Which of the following medication could he be avoiding to take?

A) Liraglutide

B) Sitagliptin

C) Dapagliflozin

D) Biguanide

E) Lisinopril

154. Following on from the previous question. Why would you not replace his current second anti diabetic with Gliclazide?

A) Gliclazide is contraindicated in this patient.

B) Gliclazide should be cautioned in those with chronic kidney disease.

C) Gliclazide is a sulfonylurea that causes weight gain.

D) Gliclazide is not licensed for Type-2 diabetes.

E) Gliclazide may cause drowsiness and not ideal for a lorry driver.

155.   What would be the best course of action for you take for Mr GH to help him better manage his type-2 Diabetes Mellitus?

A) Replace the current second anti-diabetic medication with Sitagliptin.

B) Replace the current second anti diabetic medication with Canagliflozin.

C) Increase the Metformin dose to 2 grams BD.

D) Refer the patient to the accident and emergency department.

E) Advise the patient to carry on with his current medications and remind the importance of adherence.

Simple Pharmacy Questions

1. What is Agomelatine primarily indicated for?

2. A patient has come into your pharmacy seeking advice about administering his new medication. Which part of the body is an intracavernosal injection administered to?

3. What is Alprostadil primarily indicated for?

4. What is the mode of action of Amantadine?

5. Can Aminophylline be injected intravenously?

6. Can a pregnant patient safely take Amoxicillin?

7. Is alopecia a common side effect of Anastrazole?

8. Can children under the age of 6-years take Ascorbic acid?

9. What class of antibiotic does Azithromycin belong too?

10. Is Atenolol more lipid soluble or more water soluble intrinsically in the body?

11. Which beta blocker is licensed to reverse the clinical symptoms of thyrotoxicosis?

12. Where does aldosterone act in the kidney nephron?

13. Erythropoietin is classed as a vital hormone that regulate red blood cell production. It is known to stimulate unspecialized stem cells of the bone marrow to promote the production of red blood cells. Which organ predominantly produces erythropoietin?

14. Malaria prophylaxis should be recommended to all those who are travelling to an area with high risk of malaria. Proguanil in a very common antimalarial, should it be taken weekly by an individual?

15. What does a DEXA scan assess?

16. You are carrying out a medication review in the secondary care setting for a Type-1 diabetic. He has been managing his diabetes well with short-acting and intermediate-acting insulins over the last 4 years, however due to recent poor control, the doctor has prescribed him on a trial of Pioglitazone to control his diabetes better. Are there any issues with his medications?

17. A woman of 29-years of age has been started on Simvastatin for hypercholesterolemia. Is

there any counselling that you must offer the patient when handing her the statin?

18. At the Alzheimer's society you are leading a session on dementia awareness, some of your peers are discussing the drug Donepezil. What is the mode of action of Donepezil?

19. How often should a Rivastigmine patch be replaced for a patient?

20. Rivastigmine transdermal patches administer drugs through the epidermal layers of the skin. What counselling advice should you offer to someone you dispense this medication for?

21. Patient X is taking a course of Rifampicin for Legionnaires disease. Patient X has told you that they wear daily soft contact lenses as they have quite bad vision. The trainee pharmacist asks about any counselling that you need to offer. How do you respond?

22. A discharge summary explains that a patient has Leukopenia which places the patient at a higher risk of getting an infection. Why would this be?

23. Mrs FG, a 56-year-old female is suffering from arthralgia, associated with bone pain. Her recent blood profile suggests that she has hypercalcaemia. Recently it has become unbearable and is awaking her at night. Her general practitioner has referred her for an

investigation. In the meanwhile, she has requested some pain relief. The doctor prescribes her some NSAIDs. Why should this patient not take an NSAID?

24. A female has come into you, asking for advice. She explains that her elderly father has been feeling very tired lately and has been experiencing dysuria, which is worse at night. She thinks he is suffering from dehydration. Is this the case?

25. Today you are checking a patients INR in the community anticoagulation clinic. This particular patient has been very stable on Warfarin for the last 4 years, with a 12-month time-in-range (TTR) of 89%. Today his INR reading is sub-therapeutic and below his target INR. The patient is confused as to what may have caused this result, as he has not started any new medications. Which dietary vitamin could have contributed to this?

26. You are reviewing a patient's discharge summary after their recent inpatient stay. You notice the term 'Nulliparous', what does it mean?

27. On the antenatal unit, you are reviewing a patient's drug chart. You realize that Mrs PG, who has been a sufferer of gestational hypertension, has successfully given birth to her first born in the early hours of today. She has been prescribed some opiate pain killers to help manage her pain. You also notice that her

Methyldopa must soon be stopped. How many days post-partum should it be stopped?

28. You are reviewing potentially teratogenic medications. Which antibiotic medication is contraindicated in pregnancy, especially during the first trimester, due to its anti-folate effects, which can cause foetal neural tube defects?

29. Which sodium-glucose cotransporter-2 (SGLT-2) inhibitor is licensed for use in the management of heart failure with reduced ejection fraction?

30. What counselling points would you tell a male adult patient who you supply Flucloxacillin to?

31. What would be the main advantage of using Unfractionated Heparin instead of low-molecular-weight heparin (LMWH)?

32. The community nurse has called you to inform you that she has referred her patient to urgent care as he has been experiencing melaena continually for a week since starting a new medication. What symptoms would the patient be experiencing?

33. Patient X has been prescribed a rescue prescription for Amoxicillin 500mg tablets TDS and Prednisolone 5mg tablets, 6 tablets to be taken OD for exacerbations of her croup. The patient asks how she should take the steroid

tablets as it is a lot to take in one sitting. How would you respond?

34. What is the dose of Ibuprofen for a 6-year-old child?

35. A young mother has brought in her 4-year-old son who has been suffering from an allergic reaction. You recommend her to give him Chlorphenamine to help with his symptoms. What dose should she give to her child?

36. Miss DZ, a 24-year-old female has recently given birth to her first-born daughter 2 months ago. She has come into the pharmacy today seeking emergency contraception as she had protected sex last night, but her partners condom split. After the consultation, you both decide that Levonorgestrel would be suitable for her to take. After taking the EHC, for how long should she not breast feed her daughter?

37. You are seeing to an obese woman who requires Levonorgestrel as emergency contraception. You have determined that it is suitable for to take. However, you do not make a sale to her and refer her to a prescriber. Why would you not make the sale?

38. You are a clinical pharmacist, who is carrying out a structured medication review for a patient within a general practice. What is a structured medication review?

39. Pharmacy technician TY is a male colleague who has been working in your community pharmacy for 3 years now. You are the responsible pharmacist today and notice that technician TY has taken a few tablets from the 'patient returns bin' and placed them in his pocket. You decide to confront him and report him to the GPhC. Which standard would you be complying with from the GPhC 'Standards for Pharmacy Professionals'?

40. You are overseeing a cohort of foundation year 2 junior doctors in their prescribing practise. Why should loop diuretics be avoided in women who are breast feeding?

41. A lady who has been prescribed Ezetimibe for familial hypercholesterolaemia, is asking about the mode of action of the drug, how do you respond?

42. Miss GT has flew from Ireland and forgotten her ant-epileptic medication at home. She has had yesterday's dose but has none for today and is staying in London for a week. She shows you an empty packet of her medication, it is appropriate for her to receive an emergency supply of the Lacosamide. You realise that you do not have the same brand of Lacosamide as was prescribed previously for the patient and are concerned as this drug is under a MHRA AED category. What should you do?

43. A customer has come in to purchase herbal Primrose supplements for her friend who is

currently experiencing pre-menopausal symptoms. She asks you about what menopause is?

44. Mrs DW, a 58-year-old female has come into the pharmacy wanting to complain. She believes that your pharmacy has dispensed an incorrect medication for her. You question her further to investigate this matter and find that she was supplied Sildenafil 25mg tablets. Mrs DW tells you that her husband uses this medication for his erectile dysfunction and that woman cannot use this as she does not have a penis. You explain to Mrs DW that the correct medication was supplied. For what indication could this Sildenafil be prescribed for her?

45. A female, patient believes she has a UTI, she tells you her urine is dark in colour but not odorous. She drinks lots of water and has no other symptoms. She would like to purchase cystitis treatment. Her PMR suggests that she started Ramipril 1.25 mg capsules 3 months ago, and Pioglitazone 30mg tablets 4 weeks ago. What should you do to help her?

46. Mr SD has been poorly managing his diabetes with a biguanide. The consultant has asked to trial the patient in Acarbose. What is the mode of action of this medication?

47. Mr SD is anxious about using his new medication Acarbose for his diabetes. He tells you that last time when he started taking his Metformin, he had transient diarrhoea. You are asked, how he should take the Acarbose to avoid any adverse effects?

48. You receive a prescription from the EEA, what does this acronym stand for?

49. Does finasteride have anti-androgen activity?

50. Rotigotine is a used to manage Parkinson's disease as monotherapy. How should you counsel the patient regarding sleep?

51. What is the mode of action of Norethisterone?

52. A 37-year old female with chronic myalgia who is managed by NSAID medication, has had abdominal pains that have now affected her sleep. She feels pain on the left side of her tummy, which is aggravated by food. So far antacids have not helped and since yesterday her stools are extremely dark, almost black and the patient is concerned. What action should she take?

53. You are conversing with a trainee nurse, and she asks you about the licensed clinical indication for Repaglinide. What do you tell her?

54. A care services nurse calls you seeking advice about a syringe driver. The patient who she is seeing to requires a mix of drugs administered over a period through a syringe driver. What is one advantage of using a syringe driver?

Yes / No Questions

1. Should a Risedronate 5mg dose be taken weekly?

2. Several drugs that can cross the blood-brain-barrier (BBB), tend to present adverse central nervous system affects. Would a drug have to be more hydrophilic to be able to cross the BBB readily?

3. Are Koplik spots are common symptom of dermatitis?

4. While Miss HJ was on holiday in America 2 months ago, she purchased lubricating eye drops for her dry eyes, which she used while she was out there. She has now lost the outer packaging and the bottle has no expiration date stated by the manufacturer. She asks you whether it would be ok for her to continue using it, as she only used it once?

5. Does Ulipristal acetate interrupt an existing pregnancy?

6. Malaria prophylaxis tablets Malarone® must be taken 1 to 2 days before travelling to a malaria-endemic area?

7. Your trainee technician is assessing the phlebotomy report for Mr AZ, his estimated glomerular filtration rate is 28ml/min/1.73m^2.

Does this eGFR indicates that Mr AZ has stage 4 renal impairment?

8. Miss FR has been prescribed nebulised Salbutamol for her asthma exacerbation. The respiratory nurse has advised to monitor for hyperkalaemia, as Salbutamol is commonly known to cause hyperkalaemia, is this correct?

9. Your trainee pharmacist asks if Fluoroquinolones increase the risk of tendon rupture, how would you answer?

10. Once a female who suffers from hypertension has given birth, is she able to resume with her Amlodipine antihypertensive therapy, while breastfeeding?

11. Levonorgestrel can be sold to a female of 16 years of age for use as emergency contraception?

12. A patient is unsure if she already is pregnant and is worried that if she consumes Levonorgestrel as emergency contraception, the active ingredient may interrupt the pregnancy, is this true?

13. Duty of candour relates to the ability to recognise and work within the limits of your knowledge and skills, and to refer patients when needed, is this correct?

14. A lady has come asking to purchase Hyoscine Butylbromide for gastric ulceration. Should you make the sale for this indication?

15. You are dispensing a prescription for Phenytoin and have two different brands in stock. Is it alright to dispense two different brands of Phenytoin to make up the quantity on the prescription for the patient?

16. Your trainee pharmacist is writing up a patient case study. He notes that a patient with bacterial conjunctivitis associated with pain should be treated with Chloramphenicol OTC to prevent pressurising the GP. How do you respond to this?

17. Is Fenofibrate an anticholinergic agent that can commonly cause dry mouth in elderly patients?

18. You are carrying out a medication review for a patient. They tell you that they take Nifedipine for heart failure. Is this correct?

19. Solifenacin is an agent used to treat benign prostatic hyperplasia (BPH) in males. Does it work by relaxing prostatic smooth muscle in BPH?

20. You are aware that Clonidine is a drug that belongs to a class of anti-hypertensives. Miss DV, states that she uses Clonidine for her migraines. Is this a licensed indication?

21. Switching between brands for Perampanel does not matter, when managing an epileptic patient, is this correct?

22. Can Alendronic acid be taken daily?

Mark scheme

Question number:	Answer:	Explanation:
1.	A	Option A is the correct answer, any blood pressure reading in a clinic setting between 160/100 mmHg and 180/120 mmHg would class the patient as having stage 2 hypertension. Option C and E Would be classed as Stage 3 hypertension. https://bnf.nice.org.uk/treatment-summary/hypertension.html
2.	D	Option D is the correct answer. In a clinic setting a target blood pressure below 140/90 mmHg is suggested for patients aged under 80 years. However, as Mr LK is aged over the age of 80 years a target clinic blood pressure below 150/90 mmHg would be suggested for him. This is according to the NICE NG136 guidance. However, if following the SIGN (2017), then the recommended target clinic blood pressure would be below 140/90 mmHg regardless of age.
3.	E	Option A is incorrect, she must not wait for her next annual review to get her medication reviewed or changed, and the methyldopa may start affecting her mood adversely. Option E is correct, postpartum ideally the Methyldopa must be

		stopped within 2 days after birth, as it may increase the risk of depression in the female. https://bnf.nice.org.uk/treatment-summary/hypertension.html
4.	C	Option C is the correct answer, women who are breastfeeding and require an antihypertensive, then Enalapril can be offered as a first-line to treat hypertension during the post-natal period. The mothers' active renal function and serum potassium must be monitored at regular intervals. However, it must be noted that mothers who are breastfeeding should not take ACE inhibitors or angiotensin II receptor antagonists such as Enalapril in the first few weeks after delivery, in such cases Methyldopa can be considered as an alternative.
5.	D	Option A is incorrect as the patient is already taking an angiotensin converting enzyme inhibitor (Ramipril). Option E is also incorrect as aldosterone antagonists are only licensed for use as an adjunct in resistant hypertension, not as a step 2 add-on in this scenario. Options B and C could be considered for this patient as step 2 add on antihypertensive, however as the patient has chronic heart failure, the best suited add on step 2 medication would be a thiazide-like diuretic such as Indapamide. A thiazide like diuretic would inhibit

		the Na-Cl symporter in the distal convoluted tubule, leading to decreased sodium and water reabsorption. This would lower blood pressure and offer symptomatic relief from heart failure and manage any mild fluid retention the Mr UY may have. https://bnf.nice.org.uk/treatment-summary/hypertension.html
6.	B	As Mrs SF is over the age of 55 years and not a diabetic, the first line recommended treatment for her would be a calcium Chanel blocker (CCB). Out of the options stated the only CCB suitable would be amlodipine, hence why option B is the correct answer.
7.	B	Only option B is correct. Pre-eclampsia is a disorder characterized by the elevation of blood pressure within the maternal mother. Associated symptoms may include; albuminuria, sweating, hot flushes, headaches, peripheral oedema, and excessive weight gain, palpitations, swelling and disturbed vision. Having an underlying chronic condition can increase the patients chance of developing pre-eclampsia, some examples include - renal dysfunction, diabetes, hypertension, obesity and cardiovascular conditions. Medical care and supervision is required post discharge of the mother and neonate because, as pre-

		eclampsia can leave lasting effects on both, post-birth. The neonate may experience, oxygen deprivation and growth restriction. If pre-eclampsia is not treated, it may lead to a miscarriage, convulsions, thromboembolism, stroke or even mortality.
8.	C	During the stages of pregnancy, the female may develop pre-eclampsia which is a form of severe chronic hypertension. The condition warrants immediate treatment. The first-line antihypertensive recommended during pregnancy is Labetalol hydrochloride. Labetalol crosses the placental barrier, but is not teratogenic. Hence, option C is the correct answer. Option A is the incorrect answer as it is an anti-diabetic agent, and not used to manage pre-eclampsia. The patient would be advised to lower her sodium chloride intake and not take it as a supplement to treat her hypertension, so option D is also incorrect. Bisoprolol is not indicated in gestational hypertension.
9.	A	Option A is the correct answer. Patients who are at risk of developing any hypertensive state must limit their dietary intake of sodium to no more than 2.4 grams per day. Hence why, option C is incorrect also. Option B is incorrect, the weekly alcohol intake

		must not regularly exceed 14 units per week, and the statement states that the weekly consumption must exceed 14units, which is incorrect. Option D is also incorrect, this is because to maintain a healthy weight, patients should try to keep a BMI between the ranges of 18.5 to 24.9, not 28. Salt: the facts - NHS (www.nhs.uk)
10.	B	Option C is the incorrect answer, as gentamicin is not licensed for managing psoriasis and is not orally consumed, usually topical intravenous or intramuscular administration. Option A is incorrect, fluconazole is an antifungal agent and not indicated to treat or manage psoriasis, unless a secondary infection occurs. Although coal tar is effective in minimising worsening of psoriasis, it is a topical treatment not oral, thus option E is incorrect. Option D is also incorrect, topical tacrolimus can be used in the management of flare ups. Oral preparations of tacrolimus are only licensed for use in prevention of graft rejection not psoriasis. Option B is correct, Ciclosporin is licensed for pustular psoriasis, where conventional therapy ineffective or inappropriate. https://bnf.nice.org.uk/treatment-summary/psoriasis.html
11.	B	Option B is the correct answer, this

		is because Sulfadiazine is a short-acting sulphonamide with bacteriostatic activity that is licensed for the use in preventing reoccurrence of rheumatic fever. Option A is incorrect as Hydroxyzine is a sedative antihistamine that exhibits no antibacterial activity, therefore not used in this case. Option C is also incorrect because Sulfinpyrazone is a uricosuric agent used for gouty arthritis. Option D is incorrect this is because sulfasalazine is a disease modifying anti rheumatic agent, with no antibacterial activity and thus not used to prevent rheumatic fever. Febuxostat is a xanthine oxidase inhibitor used to manage gout. https://bnf.nice.org.uk/drug/sulfadiazine.html
12.	D	Option D is the correct answer, the patient is most likely affected by an over active thyroid gland, known as hyperthyroidism. Carbimazole is used to control the overactive thyroid gland (hyperthyroidism). Carbimazole is a pro-drug, thus, after absorption the active form, Methimazole prevents thyroid peroxidase enzyme from iodinating tyrosine residues on thyroglobulin. This reduces the production of the thyroid hormones T3 and T4 (thyroxine). The patient should gain symptomatic relief. https://bnf.nice.org.uk/treatment-

		summary/hyperthyroidism.html
13.	E	Option E is the correct answer, this is because the initial scenario states that the patient is on the obstetrics unit. Although not explicitly stated, the patient is a young woman of child bearing age and at some stage of her gestation, research has suggested that Carbimazole can be teratogenic and associated with a higher risk of congenital malformations in pregnancy, especially in the first trimester. Effective contraception must be used during treatment with Carbimazole. https://www.gov.uk/drug-safety-update/carbimazole-increased-risk-of-congenital-malformations-strengthened-advice-on-contraception
14.	A	Option A is the correct answer, clinical studies have found that Propylthiouracil has a lower percentage that crosses the placenta than Carbimazole. Therefore, is preferred as an anti-thyroid drug to manage hyperthyroidism in pregnancy. Option B is incorrect as it is a transthyretin inhibitor used in polyneuropathy. Option C is also incorrect as Primidone is only indicated in the treatment of epilepsy or tremor. Option D is incorrect as Propranolol is a beta-receptor blocker not indicated for hyperthyroidism. Option E is also

		incorrect, Pyridoxine is a form of vitamin B6. https://bnf.nice.org.uk/drug/propylth iouracil.html
15.	E	Option E is the correct answer. Thyroid storm is a rare but life-threatening state of hyperthyroidism. Clinical manifestations of a thyroid storm include the above symptoms such as unexplained weight loss, hyperactivity and nausea. The most common causes of thyrotoxicosis are Graves' disease, toxic goitre and toxic adenoma. Option C is incorrect as Hashimoto's disease, is a form of chronic lymphocytic thyroiditis and does not present the above symptoms. Option A, Cushing's disease, is caused by an increase in cortisol, and associated with weight gain and fluid retention. https://bnf.nice.org.uk/treatment-summary/hypothyroidism.html https://bnf.nice.org.uk/treatment-summary/hyperthyroidism.html
16.	A	Option A is the correct answer. Drug Tariff; bulk prescription charges http://www.drugtariff.nhsbs a.nhs.uk/#/00451251-DA/DA00450845/9, Royal Pharmaceutical Society. The Administration and Control of Medicines in Care Homes and Children services 2003.
17.	E	Option E is the correct answer. All

	C	bulk prescriptions cannot be transmitted electronically. Drug Tariff; bulk prescription charges http://www.drugtariff.nhsbsa.nhs.uk/#/00451251-DA/DA00450845/9, Royal Pharmaceutical Society. The Administration and Control of Medicines in Care Homes and Children services 2003.
18.	E	Option E is the correct answer, Domperidone is a Prescription Only Medicines (POM), such medications cannot be issued by bulk prescription. Drug Tariff; bulk prescription charges http://www.drugtariff.nhsbsa.nhs.uk/#/00451251-DA/DA00450845/9, Royal Pharmaceutical Society. The Administration and Control of Medicines in Care Homes and Children services 2003.
19.	E	Option E is the correct answer, bulk prescribing is not dealt with electronically. Therefore, paper is used for prescribing and not saved. Drug Tariff; bulk prescription charges http://www.drugtariff.nhsbsa.nhs.uk/#/00451251-DA/DA00450845/9, Royal Pharmaceutical Society. The Administration and Control of Medicines in Care Homes and Children services 2003.
20.	C	Option C is the correct answer, a child aged between 2 to 3 years

		should be given a dose of 180 mg to be given every 4-6 hours. https://bnf.nice.org.uk/drug/paracetamol.html
21.	A	Option A is incorrect as the matter should not be left for others to deal with. You must deal with it yourself otherwise it may get forgotten about. Option C in incorrect as you should follow the 'no blame culture' and try to explain to the consultant about this, complaining would escalate the matter too soon. Option D is also incorrect, as the patient may not be entirely aware or competent. However, it is important to engage patients and provide patient centred care. Option B is the best course of action to take as it will ensure that the patient is not given the incorrect medication and a correct one is given.
22.	E	Option E is the correct answer, shingles is of viral origin which corresponds to infected nerves. These nerve sites can occur anywhere within the skin, and around the body. Moreover, pain, pins and needles sensation may occur and this may change the sensation of the skin and precipitate itching occur.
23.	D	Option D is the correct answer, Human Resources and recruitment is not a part of clinical governance. https://www.england.nhs.uk/mat-

		transformation/matrons-handbook/governance-patient-safety-and-quality/
24.	E	Option E is the correct answer, Sulfasalazine is an Aminosalicylate that can cause blood disorders. Miss WP should be advised to report any unexplained bleeding, bruising, purpura, sore throat, fever or malaise that occurs during treatment. https://bnf.nice.org.uk/drug/sulfasalazine.html
25.	C	Option C is the correct answer, Patients should be advised to look for any report any signs of haematuria, dysuria, or urinary urgency during treatment. As the risk of bladder cancer does increase. https://bnf.nice.org.uk/drug/pioglitazone.html#patientAndCarerAdvice
26.	C	Option C is the correct answer, Higher doses of statins are associated with muscle breakdown and degradation. Therefore, patients must be advised to look out for signs of myopathy, myalgia and pain. https://bnf.nice.org.uk/drug/atorvastatin.html
27.	D	Option D is the correct answer. Evidence suggests that those patients who are over the age of 60 years have an increased risk of developing ventricular arrhythmia due to the QT-interval elongating. If

		such symptoms occur, then the Domperidone must be stopped.
28.	C	Option C is the correct answer, patients who take Coumarin such as Warfarin are at an increased risk of bleeding, therefore those who experience a high (sub therapeutic) INR would be at a higher risk of getting bleeds and haematuria. All the other adverse effects stated are not commonly associated with Warfarin. https://bnf.nice.org.uk/drug/warfarin -sodium.html
29.	D	Option D is the correct answer. Rivaroxaban is a direct oral anticoagulant which selectively blocks factor XA, this intern interrupts the coagulation cascade through the intrinsic and extrinsic pathway. Thus, thins the blood. Warfarin is also an anticoagulant, but it acts as a vitamin-K antagonist, so is the incorrect answer. Ticagrelor is a P2Y12 receptor antagonist that prevents platelet activation and aggregation, so an incorrect option. Doxazosin and Lisinopril are both anti-hypertensives. https://www.medicines.org.uk/emc/ product/2793/smpc#gref
30.	D	Option D is the correct answer, beta blockers such as Bisoprolol are associated with weight gain. Evidence has suggested that beta blockers can lower rates of

		metabolism. This, reduces rates of endurance and exercise tolerance. Amlodipine can increase weight by causing fluid accumulation in the lower limbs, but this patient has not experienced this, therefore it is the incorrect option. Metformin is usually associated with weight loss not weight gain, so it is also the incorrect option. https://www.medicines.org.uk/emc/product/8850/smpc
31.	C	Option C is the correct answer. Amiodarone is an iodine-rich antiarrhythmic agent that causes a cutaneous photosensitivity reaction. This can be associated with a peculiar blue-gray discoloration of the skin. Patients must be advised to avoid prolonged skin exposure and use adequate sun protection to avoid this reaction. Symptoms of photosensitivity may include burning, stinging and redness of the skin associated with urticaria. https://www.medicines.org.uk/emc/product/6018/smpc#gref
32.	A	Option A is the correct answer. Angiotensin converting enzyme inhibitors such as Lisinopril can cause accumulation of bradykinin in the respiratory cavity which can leave to a low level chronic dry cough. In some patients the cough may be transient, in others it can become chronic and really affect their lifestyle. In such patients the

		medication should be switched to an alternative antihypertensive. https://bnf.nice.org.uk/drug/lisinopril.html
33.	E	Option E is the correct answer. An antiplatelet such as Ticagrelor would be prescribed in combination with Aspirin. It is licensed for the prevention of atherothrombotic events in patients with acute coronary syndrome; the combination is usually given for up to 12 months. After which the Ticagrelor treatment ceases. https://bnf.nice.org.uk/treatment-summary/antiplatelet-drugs.html
34.	E	Option E is the correct answer, out of all the medications stated Rifampicin and its metabolites are known to colour the urine, saliva, sweat, tears and faeces to an orange-red colour. Such counselling points are vital to be conveyed across to patients as it can cause a great deal of anxiety for both patients and medical professionals. https://bnf.nice.org.uk/drug/rifampicin.html
35.	B	Option B is the correct answer. NICE guidelines recommend that patients are offered an anticoagulant, as Warfarin is the only anticoagulant listed then that would be the correct option. Aspirin is now longer recommended for reducing stroke risk in patients with

		AF. Doctors have always thought carefully about the risk/benefit profile of starting someone on Warfarin. A history of falls, old age, alcohol excess and a history of previous bleeding are common things that make us consider whether warfarin is in the best interests of the patient. NICE now recommend we formalise this risk assessment using the HASBLED scoring system.
36.	C	Option C is correct. For a chest related infection, usually Amoxicillin or Co-Amoxiclav are indicted as first-line. However, this patient has a penicillin allergy therefore, a macrolide would be best suited such as Clarithromycin. A Cephalosporin may be used, but for those patients with a true penicillin allergy, sometimes a Cephalosporin may cause sensitivity in some patients. So best avoided. https://pathways.nice.org.uk/pathways/respiratory-conditions/respiratory-infections
37.	D	Option D is the correct answer. Diabetic patients should be advised to carry a source of fast release glucose such as sweets. Chocolates contain more fat than sweets, therefore this can slow down the absorption of glucose into the blood stream. Therefore, sweets are preferred over chocolate due to their absorption

		rate. https://www.diabetes.co.uk/food/lo w-sugar-sweets-and-treats.html
38.	D	Option D is the correct answer. Vitamin A is best avoided in high doses at any stage of the pregnancy as it can have teratogenic effects. https://www.nhs.uk/conditions/vita mins-and-minerals/vitamin-a/
39.	C	Option C is the correct answer. Rickets can sometimes have a genetic component, however very commonly it is causing the softening and weakening of bones in children, this usually precipitated by an extreme and prolonged vitamin D deficiency. https://www.nhs.uk/conditions/ricke ts-and-osteomalacia/causes/
40.	B	Option B is the correct answer. Colic has unknown aetiology, however several factors are known to contribute to it, such as wind, hormones and over sensitivity of the digestive system. Colic usually subsides by the time the baby is 3 months of age. However, if colic persists, it could be due to intolerance to milk formula or other underlying conditions. https://www.nhs.uk/conditions/colic /
41.	D	Option D is the correct answer, this disperses and prevents gas bubbles from forming in the gastrointestinal tract and can

		alleviate symptoms of colic. Simethicone is usually licensed for children over the age of 1 month. https://bnf.nice.org.uk/drug/simeticone.html
42.	D	Option D is the correct answer. Lactulose is indicated as a first line treatment. Lactulose is not known to be harmful to a foetus as per evidence-based animal studies. Enoxaparin is an anticoagulant that is not needed for constipation and is not available OTC. Codeine is also not a laxative. Senna and Bisacodyl tablets can be harsh during a pregnancy, therefore not recommended during pregnancy. https://www.medicines.org.uk/emc/product/2796/smpc#gref
43.	D	Option D is the correct answer, Misoprostol is contraindicated in pregnancy. For those women wishing to conceive and carry a child, there must avoid this drug as it may abort the child. https://bnf.nice.org.uk/drug/misoprostol.html
44.	E	Option E is the correct answer. Quetiapine is licensed in the treatment of mania in bipolar disorder. https://bnf.nice.org.uk/drug/quetiapine.html#indicationsAndDoses
45.	F	Option F is the correct answer. Insulin glargine is produced by recombinant DNA technology using a non-pathogenic laboratory strain

		of Escherichia coli. https://www.medicines.org.uk/emc/ product/2376/smpc#gref
46.	C	Option C is the correct option. The most common manifestation of impaired macrovascular function in diabetes mellitus is cardiovascular atherosclerosis, microvascular dysfunction leads to nephropathy and retinopathy. Thus, in diabetes you must monitor for the changes in the microvasculature to assess risk of ischemia.
47.	C	Option A is false because Methadone can be administered up to twice daily, however, should not exceed a BD dosing regimen due to risk of accumulation. Option B is false, as hyperhidrosis (excessive sweating) is a very common side effect of methadone. Option D is incorrect, as methadone has a tendency to elongate the cardiac Q-T interval, regular ECG monitoring is vital. Option E is also incorrect because hypothyroidism would require a dose reduction, not an increase in the dose of Methadone, as the residual rate of metabolism is reduced in the individual. Hence, option C is correct. https://bnf.nice.org.uk/treatment-summary/analgesics.html https://bnf.nice.org.uk/drug/methadone-hydrochloride.html
48.	B	Option B is the correct answer, this

		is because any drug which promotes teratogenicity causes an abnormality following foetal exposure during pregnancy. Teratogens are usually discovered after an increased prevalence of a particular birth defect. https://bnf.nice.org.uk/treatment-summary/contraceptives-hormonal.html
49.	D	Option A and B is incorrect; this is because combined oral contraceptives that contain a fixed amount of an oestrogen and a progestogen are called monophasic; however, those with varying amounts of the two hormones are called multiphasic. Option C is incorrect because a monophasic combined oral contraceptive has oestrogen and progestogen, not oestrogen only as stated in the answer option. Option E is incorrect as a combined pill only has 2 active hormonal ingredients, not 3. Thus, option D is correct. https://bnf.nice.org.uk/treatment-summary/contraceptives-hormonal.html
50.	B	All the options are true except option B. The patient's plasma glycaemic control is not necessarily required to be reviewed annually. Birth control containing oestrogen can increase blood pressure. When women who have high blood pressure use these birth control

		methods, they have an increased risk of stroke and heart attack compared with women who do not have high blood pressure. https://bnf.nice.org.uk/treatment-summary/contraceptives-hormonal.html
51.	D	Option D is the correct answer. This is because patients taking oral contraceptives have an increased risk of postoperative venous thromboembolism because of the combined effects of hormones and the hypercoagulable state, which accompanies surgical stress and postoperative immobility. Thus, the combined oral contraceptive must be stopped at least 4 weeks prior to surgery. https://www.ncbi.nlm.nih.gov/pmc/articles/PMC3025411/
52.	E	Option E is the correct answer, Estrone is a type of oestrogen that would not be contained as an active ingredient in a progestogen only contraceptive. Etonogestral is an implant form of progestogen, which primarily suppresses ovulation and provides highly effective contraception for up to 3 years. https://journals.rcni.com/nursing-standard/undertaking-an-oral-contraceptive-pill-review-ns.2017.e10966
53.	C	Option A is true this is because women using progestogen only

		contraceptives over the age of 50 years are at an increased risk of developing cancer related conditions. Option B is also true, as studies have suggested that progesterone was reported to reduce cortical bone loss. Option D is also true, as patients who have osteoporosis should consider alternative progestogen only preparations. Option E is also true as progestogen only preparations can increase risk of having a thromboembolic event. Thus, Option C is the correct option, and the statement is false. After discontinuation of a depot medroxyprogesterone acetate injection, female fertility is not returned for up to a year after, not 'at least a year', therefore it is possible to get pregnant within the 12 months of stopping the injection. https://bnf.nice.org.uk/treatment-summary/contraceptives-interactions.html
54.	C	Option A is incorrect because Carbamazepine is an enzyme inducer not inhibitor, thus it decreases the concentration of drugs which are concomitantly administered. Option B is also incorrect, whether Miss WR is taking the Carbamazepine for short term or long-term basis, she is still at risk of getting pregnant, therefore for the short-term basis,

		and she must be advised to use a barrier method until her contraception is sorted. Option D is true, but the incorrect option, because it is unlicensed to use tricyclic regimens with a shorter 4-day tablet free interval. Pharmacists should not recommend unlicensed medications to patients without the recommendation of a doctor. Option E is also false because Ulipristal acetate presents with a lower plasma concentration when taken with an enzyme inducer such as Carbamazepine. Option C is the correct option, the statement is true because patients who are initiated on a long-term enzyme inducer are best advised to use a parenteral progestogen contraceptive such as medroxyprogesterone or an IUD. https://bnf.nice.org.uk/treatment-summary/emergency-contraception.html
55.	A	Option A is correct; this is because the effectivity of the Ulipristal acetate may be all altered as a result. Miss YT should wait 5 days after taking Ulipristal acetate before starting suitable hormonal contraception; she must use condoms or abstain from intercourse during the 5-day waiting period. Option B is incorrect, as the Ulipristal may lose its effectivity. Option C, D and E is false.

		https://bnf.nice.org.uk/drug/uliprista l-acetate.html
56.	A	Option A is the correct answer, emergency contraception should be offered to those women who have unprotected intercourse from day 5 after abortion, miscarriage, ectopic pregnancy. Options B and C are incorrect as the patient does NOT require emergency contraception as she is still within the 5-day period post-procedure. Options D and E are also incorrect, this is because the post procedural period is of 5 days, anything beyond the 5 days would require emergency contraception. https://bnf.nice.org.uk/treatment-summary/obstetrics.html
57.	D	Option A in incorrect, this is because with every passing day the effectivity of Levonorgestrel decreases, as the intercourse was almost 3 days ago and the patient is obese, there is a high chance that the Levonorgestrel may not provide adequate contraceptive protection. Option B is incorrect, this is because it is unlicensed to sell 2 Levonorgestrel tablets and to double the dose without the guidance of a prescriber. Therefore, also guidelines may suggest this, OTC is not recommended. Option C is incorrect, because you can supply the patient with Ulipristal acetate as a form of emergency

		contraception, therefore option D is correct. Option E is also incorrect because short acting insulins or patient with Type-1 Diabetes are not contraindicated with Levonorgestrel or Ulipristal acetate. https://bnf.nice.org.uk/drug/uliprista l-acetate.html
58.	E	Option E is the correct answer. If a patient has not been assessed prior to commencing iron deficiency treatment for anaemia, then an OTC sale would not be appropriate. In this scenario, as the patient is male, it is not possible for him to have lost blood/iron through menstruation. Therefore, it is vital that any serious underlying cause of the anaemia is ruled out (e.g, gastric erosion, and gastro-intestinal cancer). https://bnf.nice.org.uk/treatment-summary/anaemia-iron-deficiency.html
59.	C	Option C is the correct answer, the oral dose of elemental iron for iron-deficiency anaemia should be 100 to 200□mg daily. https://bnf.nice.org.uk/treatment-summary/anaemia-iron-deficiency.html
60.	C	Option C is the correct answer. Ascorbic acid is also known as vitamin C, it is a water-soluble vitamin th increases the absorption and uptake of basic iron molecules

		which are not heme bound. Ascorbic acid reduces the iron to facilitate better iron absorption from the gastrointestinal tract. https://bnf.nice.org.uk/treatment-summary/anaemia-iron-deficiency.html
61.	B	Option A is incorrect, this is because parenteral iron therapy can be suggested for patients intolerant or unresponsive to oral iron therapy, for use in treating functional iron deficiency, or acute non-functional iron deficiency anaemia also. Should there be a medically justified need for a pregnant patient to take iron parenterally, then they can during second and third trimester, thus option C is incorrect. Option E is also incorrect as parenteral iron has not shown to impair fertility. Option B is correct and option D is incorrect. This is because the absorption of oral iron is reduced when administered concomitantly with parenteral iron preparations. https://bnf.nice.org.uk/drug/ferric-carboxymaltose.html
62.	A	Option A is the false statement thus, is the correct answer. Although iron tablets are best absorbed on an empty stomach, they can be taken with food also. All the other statements are true, loss of appetite would require referral to be seen by a doctor as it may suggest a differing diagnosis.

		https://bnf.nice.org.uk/drug/ferrous-sulfate.html
63.	B	Option B is correct; hypoglycaemia is not an associated side effect. Several hours after ingestion, the shock phase can become manifest. Higher levels of iron irritate the gastrointestinal mucosa, the increase in iron uptake causes inadequate perfusion. This results in cellular toxicity and multiorgan failure develops. Symptoms such as hypotension, tachycardia and seizures, metabolic acidosis, renal failure, hepatic failure, and functional myocardial depression can occur. https://bnf.nice.org.uk/treatment-summary/anaemia-iron-deficiency.html
64.	A	Option A is the correct answer. The presence of protein in the urine is a sign of degeneration of the following glomerular structural layers, such as the glomerular endothelial cell, the basement membrane, and the visceral epithelial cell. A sign of progressive renal dysfunction. With proteinuria the eGFR would usually decrease over time. After glomerular filtration, the filtrate is produced and reabsorbed, throughout the nephrons but proteinuria is not independent of GFR. Proteinuria is not associated with hepatic function; only renal function and it can be classed as a profound

		symptom of progressive diabetic control decline.
65.	C	Option A is incorrect, although national guidelines state that alcohol intake should be up to 14 units per week, this does not necessarily mean that she should 'increase' her weekly alcohol intake to bring it up to 14 units per week. Miss RQ should decrease intake of saturated fats, not increase it, as a higher intake of it would increase the patients overall low-density lipoprotein within the plasma, thus option B is incorrect. Option D is also incorrect because fasting and decreasing calorie intake is not recommended in diabetic patients due to risk of hypoglycaemia. Option E is also incorrect as there is no evidence that suggest that alternative 'diabetic friendly/low sugar' foods or snacks are better for diabetics, because they usually have higher fat content thus, not a good alternative. Option C is correct, patients should aim for a gradual weight decrease between 5% to 10% of their body weight over a period. https://www.nice.org.uk/guidance/ng28/ifp/chapter/diet-and-lifestyle
66.	A	Option A is correct, the most recent guidance from the DVLA states that if the blood-glucose is less than 4 mmol/litre, then she must not drive. Thus, in the option it states that if her blood plasma level

		is 3.9mmol/litre then she must not drive. Option B is incorrect, NICE guidance suggests that Blood-glucose should always be above 5 mmol/litre while driving, to ensure optimum glycaemic control in maintained. Option C is incorrect, if Miss RQ has a plasma glucose level of 5.9mmol/litre, then that is adequate enough to carry on driving, and does not require her to stop driving unless experiencing episodes of hypoglycaemia. Option D is also incorrect as all diabetics are recommended to carry glucose snacks especially when they experience episodes of hypoglycaemia, to counteract it. Option E is incorrect as DVLA guidance does not require information on hypoglycaemic episodes to be passed over. https://www.gov.uk/diabetes-driving
67.	B	Option B is the correct answer, the patient is currently experiencing an episode of hypoglycaemia. Signs of low blood sugar include trembling, feeling weak and blurred vision. This can then lead to excessive sweating. The patient is not experiencing hyperglycaemia as the patient has not had any symptoms of high blood sugar, increased thirst and/or hunger, blurred vision, increase in frequent urination or headache.

		https://www.diabetes.org.uk/guide-to-diabetes/complications/hypers?gclid=Cj0KCQiAhMOMBhDhARIsAPVml
68.	A	Option A is the correct answer, according to the 'Driver and Vehicle Licensing Agency', recommendations suggest that the diabetic driver must consume sufficient glucose to ensure that the plasma glucose control is above 5 mmol/litre. The recommended time is 45 minutes after ingestion of adequate glucose. The diabetic patient must remove themselves from the driver's seat, so that they do not affect the car in any way, sometimes a hypoglycaemic attack may cause tremors/seizures which may affects the controls of the car. Thus, it is best to be away from the driver's seat. https://www.gov.uk/diabetes-driving
69.	E	Option E is the correct answer. With an oral glucose tolerance test, a blood sample will be collected when the patient arrives. This would be the fasting blood glucose value. It provides a baseline for comparing other glucose values. The patient will be asked to drink a measured amount of glucose, usually 75 grams or 100 grams. Blood samples will be collected at a timed interval of 2 hours after

		having drank the glucose. https://bnf.nice.org.uk/treatment-summary/diabetes.html
70.	D	Option D is the correct answer, this is because Mr AX is currently on dual anti-diabetic therapy, in such a patient when two or more antidiabetic drugs are prescribed, the HbA1c concentration target should be 53 mmol/mol. A lower HbA1c target of 48 mmol/mol would only be recommended if Mr AX's type 2 diabetes was managed by diet and lifestyle or when combined with a single antidiabetic drug (not one that is classed as a hypoglycaemia causing agent such as Gliclazide). https://bnf.nice.org.uk/treatment-summary/type-2-diabetes.html
71.	B	Option B is the correct answer, this is because even though all Sulfonylurea drugs are associated with hypoglycaemia, as Mrs JB has renal impairment, this would only prolong the clearance of the Sulfonylurea, thus increase its effects and having a higher incidence of hypoglycaemic episodes. In such a patient, it is recommended to give a short acting Sulfonylurea. Hence why, Gliclazide would be best tolerated. Option E is incorrect as Pioglitazone is not a Sulfonylurea. https://bnf.nice.org.uk/treatment-summary/type-2-diabetes.html

72.	D	Option D is the correct answer, the patient has been experiencing severe adverse effects ever since she started taking the new medication. This is a sign of her not tolerating the Metformin well. She must not suffer in silence and get this addressed as soon as possible. It may require an alternate form of the Metformin such a prolonged release preparation or an alternate drug completely. Hence why all the other options may be considered when dealing with Miss BM, but not option E. https://bnf.nice.org.uk/treatment-summary/type-2-diabetes.html
73.	B	Option B is the correct answer, as it is the only GLP-1 receptor agonist available. Repaglinide is a secretagogue like sulfonylureas, although not structurally related, it induces insulin secretion from pancreas. All the other options stated are Sulfonylureas, option A (Vildagliptin) which is a DPP4-inhibitor.
74.	C	Option C is the correct answer, this is because insulin Degludec is a long-acting insulin, therefore must be injected once daily according to the patient's requirements, to maintain basal insulin levels. Not with every main meal. The insulin Aspart is a rapid acting insulin, therefore, is not injected once daily to maintain basal levels, but

		instead should ideally be injected immediately before meals, in response to glucose absorbed from a meal. Option A is incorrect as the patient is mistaken about both the insulin's and must be advised accordingly to ensure they do not misuse the insulin. Option B is incorrect as insulin Aspart is not an intermediate acting insulin. Option D is incorrect, although insulin Degludec would be formulated as a soluble insulin, it is only injected once daily, not twice daily. https://bnf.nice.org.uk/treatment-summary/insulin-2.html
75.	E	All statements stated are correct about managing diabetic ketoacidosis, however, option E is false. Thus, the correct answer. Salbutamol is not administrated to the patient while managing diabetic ketoacidosis. Option C is true because diabetic ketoacidosis is caused by the body being deficient of insulin. https://bnf.nice.org.uk/treatment-summary/diabetic-ketoacidosis.html
76.	A	Option A is the correct answer. Peak flow is the maximum volume of air that can be expelled from the lung's cavity during a vigorous exhalation. Within a clinical setting, peak flow determines the degree of respiratory impairment in patients with obstructive lung diseases, such as asthma in Mr XC. Thus,

		having a peak flow reading between Peak flow >☐50-75% would indicate the patient has moderate acute asthma. https://bnf.nice.org.uk/treatment-summary/asthma-acute.html
77.	E	Option E is the correct answer. Should a patient have an arterial oxygen saturation of (SpO2) <☐92%; then this calls for emergency treatment and is classed as life threatening asthma.
78.	D	Option D is the correct answer, hypertension is not an associated symptom of life-threatening asthma, but hypotension is. In such a situation, breathing rate drops, heart rate decreases and ultimately so does arterial blood pressure.
79.	C	Occlusion of the coronary artery is the correct answer. This is because in a STEMI, a haemorrhaged or occluded artery leads to extensive cardiac damage. Unstable angina is the incorrect answer because it is a classic sign of a non-ST segment elevation myocardial infarction. This may often lead to a STEMI is left untreated. An occluded peripheral vein or hypertension would primarily lead to an embolism/DVT/clot but not necessarily be the primary cause of a STEMI. Pulmonary oedema is usually a complication of a myocardial infarction, however, is

		not a cause of a STEMI. Usually associated with heart failure, linked to valvular malfunction. https://bnf.nice.org.uk/treatment-summary/acute-coronary-syndromes.html
80.	A	The correct answer is to restore the cardiac blood flow as soon as possible to prevent structural damages to the heart muscle. Although it would be beneficial to see a reduction of protein T troponin levels in the blood, it is not a primary focus when managing a STEMI. Not restoring cardiac blood flow by not appropriately managing the occluded artery/vein would lead to eventual mortality. Increasing arterial blood pressure would only add pressure to the struggling heart muscle and cause further stress, thus is the incorrect answer. Restoring glomerular or hepatic blood flow has no relevance to the primary management of an ACS. https://bnf.nice.org.uk/treatment-summary/acute-coronary-syndromes.html
81.	B	All patient having an MI managed while admitted in hospital must be monitored for hyperglycaemia. Hyperglycaemia can also occur when normal hormonal control of blood glucose concentration is disturbed by the stress associated with acute myocardial infarction. The blood glucose is raised in the immediate period following

		acute myocardial infarction irrespective of diabetes status. Should the patient be hyperglycaemic then the patient should receive an infusion of insulin to counteract the high plasma glucose levels. https://bnf.nice.org.uk/treatment-summary/acute-coronary-syndromes.html
82.	C	Out of all the statements stated, the only correct statement is for Mr AC to stop smoking. Smoking cessation for this patient who presented with an acute myocardial infarction, represents an important modifiable risk factor for recurrent events. Smoking cessation decreases the risk of recurrent cardiovascular events and mortality by 30%. A BMI under $18kg/m^2$ is not healthy and the patient would be classed as underweight. Plasma LDL levels must be lowered, while HDL levels must be increased so option A is also incorrect. Mr AC should by advised that his weekly alcohol intake should be no more than 14 units per week according to current national recommendations. Skipping meals regularly would not be recommended when trying to maintain optimum glycaemic controls. https://bnf.nice.org.uk/treatment-summary/acute-coronary-syndromes.html

83.	C	Triple therapy (2 antiplatelet drugs and an anticoagulant) can be used and is recommended as an option for preventing atherothrombotic events following an ACS with those patients who have elevated cardiac biomarkers such a troponin T. Aspirin must be continued indefinitely following an ACS event. Dual antiplatelet therapy (aspirin with a second antiplatelet) should be continued for up to 12 months unless contraindicated. Subcutaneous / intravenous heparins are not indicated to be used indefinitely. Diltiazem and Verapamil are indicated for those patients who do not have pulmonary congestion and used as an alternative to beta blockers. https://bnf.nice.org.uk/treatment-summary/cardiovascular-disease-risk-assessment-and-prevention.html
84.	D	Option D is the correct answer, this is because the parameters stated in the scenario are all high-risk factors. The patient is over the age of 75-years, has an impaired immune system due to long term steroid therapy and has a history of parenteral drug use. Also, the fact that the patient had cyanosis of the lips, places this patient in the high-risk group for sepsis.
85.	A	Option A is the correct option. Not passing urine in the previous 8 hours is not clinically an alarming

		symptom of sepsis. However, should the patient not pass any urine in the past 12-18 hours, then this would be classed as a high-risk symptom. The other clinical parameters stated are all high-risk factors. https://www.nice.org.uk/guidance/ng51/chapter/Recommendations
86.	B	Option B is the correct answer, a reduced heart rate would mean that the child is at high risk of sepsis because, the decreased blood pressure would lead to a series of harmful complications: Blood flow decreases to vital organs. The heart attempts to compensate by working harder, increasing the heart rate and the amount of blood pumped. The other symptoms stated are not classed as high-risk factors. https://www.nice.org.uk/guidance/ng51/chapter/Recommendations
87.	A	Option A is the correct answer, patients taking immunosuppressant drugs such as Methotrexate tend to have an impaired/weaker immune system. Therefore, are more prone to contract sepsis. Another factor in which Methotrexate may promote sepsis is via renal dysfunction causing accumulation. This would result in pancytopenia and making the patient susceptible to infections and severe sepsis ultimately. Methotrexate is considered as a

		first-line disease-modifying anti-rheumatic agent. https://www.nice.org.uk/guidance/ng51/chapter/Recommendations
88.	B	Option B is the correct answer, Nitrofurantoin is recommended as a first line treatment for uncomplicated UTI's. Trimethoprim would be considered as a second line treatment, if no improvement in lower UTI symptoms on first choice taken for at least 48 hours, or when first choice is not suitable. Gentamicin is usually parenteral or topical and not ingested orally. Metronidazole and Co-Amoxiclav are not recommended first line antibiotics for UTI's. https://www.nice.org.uk/guidance/ng109
89.	A	Option A is correct, if the estimated glomerular filtration rate [eGFR] is 45 ml/minute or less, then Nitrofurantoin is not suitable. It may be used with caution if eGFR is between 30–44mL/ minute/1.73m^2 as a short-course treatment of up to 7 days, for uncomplicated lower urinary-tract infections. https://bnf.nice.org.uk/drug/nitrofurantoin.html#renalImpairment
90.	C	Option C is the correct answer, evidence has shown that Nitrofurantoin affects urine culture and can present with a false positive urine glucose test. Ideally the test must be postponed.

		https://bnf.nice.org.uk/drug/nitrofur antoin.html#renalImpairment
91.	E	Option E is the correct answer. Confusion, Urea nitrogen level raised over 7 mmol/litre in the blood, Respiratory rate (of 30 breaths per minute or more), and Blood pressure lower than 60 mmHg (diastolic) / 90 mmHg (systolic), Age 65 years or more. A patient with Pneumonia, when presented at the hospital, must be assessed by a healthcare professional for their risk of death. This is calculated using the CURB65 score, classed at low, intermediate, or high risk. Each parameter is given 1 point for each of the following prognostic features. https://www.nice.org.uk/guidance/q s110/chapter/quality-statement-4-mortality-risk-assessment-in-hospital-using-curb65-score
92.	D	Option D is the correct answer. Any score between 3 and 5 would place a risk of more than 15% mortality for the patient. A score between 0 to 1 places the patient at a low risk with less than 3% mortality risk. A score of 2 places the patient at an intermediate risk 3-15% mortality risk. https://www.nice.org.uk/guidance/q s110/chapter/quality-statement-4-mortality-risk-assessment-in-hospital-using-curb65-score

93.	B	Option B is the correct answer, Clarithromycin is only indicated for moderate to severe community acquired pneumonia. As the patient has a low severity risk, Amoxicillin would be indicated. Metronidazole is not indicated for pneumonia. Co-Amoxiclav is indicated for pneumonia but for those who have a high death risk, so not the correct answer. https://www.nice.org.uk/guidance/ng138
94.	D	Option D is the correct answer, the patient has presented with adverse effects of Carbimazole. An additional OTC preparation would only mask symptoms of an underlying cause which must be addressed before issuing any further medication. The patient must stop taking her Carbimazole and be referred for medical attention. Carbamazepine is not indicated in hyperthyroidism. Therefore, option B is incorrect. https://bnf.nice.org.uk/drug/carbimazole.html
95.	C	Option C is the correct option. Patients who experience symptoms of heart burn, should be advised to consume their evening meal or food at least 3-4 hours before going to bed. The patient should avoid to eat a big meal before bed, as this may can promote indigestion. If Mr GY would eat a large meal and then

		immediately get in bed, laying horizontally could cause acid reflux, symptoms of which include heartburn, trouble swallowing and night-time asthma. All the other options stated are correct and appropriate advice to give the patient. https://bnf.nice.org.uk/treatment-summary/dyspepsia.html
96.	A	Option A is the correct answer, GORD may occur with or without oesophageal inflammation, resulting from the reflux of gastric contents into the oesophagus. Option B is incorrect as the symptoms of abdominal distention suggest some sort of abdominal distention. Option C suggests abnormal bile transportation and intestinal obstruction. Option D is also incorrect, the synonyms suggests that the patient is suffering from gastroenteritis, potentially of bacterial origin. Option E suggests red flag symptoms which suggests some sort of malignancy such as Oesophageal cancer. https://cks.nice.org.uk/topics/gord-in-children/diagnosis/differential-diagnosis-red-flag-features/ https://bnf.nice.org.uk/treatment-summary/dyspepsia.html
97.	E	Making an OTC sale would not be appropriate in this patient, this would only mask the symptoms which are being caused by a more

			sinister cause. The patient should be referred for an urgent medical investigation, such as endoscopy. This is usually recommended for patients such as Mrs SV who is over the age of 55 years with unexplained weight loss and symptoms of upper abdominal pain, reflux, or dyspepsia. Therefore, Option E is correct. Option B is also correct, but not the first-line step to take. Although smoking cessation would benefit this patient, she first needs an urgent, medical investigation to rule out any malignancy. https://bnf.nice.org.uk/treatment-summary/dyspepsia.html https://www.nice.org.uk/guidance/conditions-and-diseases/cancer/oesophageal-cancer
98.	B		The patient has already had a gastroscopy carried out, which is the same as an endoscopy, so option A is incorrect. Gastroenteritis usually is an infection of bacterial or viral origin, therefore a rapid stool test can detect rotavirus or norovirus, but a full-blood count would not test for viruses that cause gastroenteritis, so option D is incorrect. Option C is not a diagnostic test, it is only looking for 1 symptom of distention or lumps. Option E is not applicable for this scenario, as an oral glucose tolerance test

		measures your body's response too glucose to screen for Type-2 Diabetes, none of the patient's symptoms relate to diabetes. Option B is the correct answer, The presence of H. pylori can be confirmed by a Urea 13C breath test. The patient already prevents symptoms of a H.Pylori Infection. The patient would ingest some urea labelled non-radioactive carbon-13. After some time, the detection of isotope-labelled CO_2 in exhaled breath indicates that the urea was split; this indicates that the urease enzyme form H. pylori is present in the stomach's cavity and hence that H.Pylori bacteria are present. https://bnf.nice.org.uk/treatment-summary/helicobacter-pylori-infection.html
99.	D	Option D is the correct answer, as omeprazole is a PPI, it must be stopped before a gastroscopic procedure as it may mask symptoms of cancer. Thus, would render the gastroscopy useless. Option A and E are incorrect as both medications stated are H-2 antagonists. Calcium carbonate is an antacid and Bismuth subsalicylate can be classed as an antacid not a PPI. https://www.prescqipp.info/umbrac o/surface/authorisedmediasurface/i ndex?url=%2fmedia%2f1646%2fb9 2-safety-of-long-term-ppis-21.pdf

100.	A	Option A is the correct answer, it is important to remain upright as laying down would cause oesophageal irritation. The patient must be advised to report any oral symptoms such as (oesophagitis, oesophageal ulcers, oesophageal stricture, and oesophageal erosions) must be reported and seek medical attention. Other associated symptoms include dysphagia, worsening heartburn, pain, or retrosternal pain. Option D is incorrect as the duration to remain upright is not long enough, it must be at least 30 minutes as stated in option A. Option E is incorrect as Alendronic acid should be taken on an empty stomach https://bnf.nice.org.uk/drug/alendronic-acid.html
101.	D	Option D is the correct answer, the reduced ejection fraction happens when the muscle of the left ventricle is not pumping as well as normal. The ejection fraction is 40% or less. The amount of blood being pumped out of the heart is less than the body needs. Option B is incorrect because reduced ejection fraction is caused at the left ventricle, not the right. https://bnf.nice.org.uk/treatment-summary/chronic-heart-failure.html
102.	A	Option A is the correct answer. Patients who have heart failure with a reduced ejection fraction should start treatment with a

		licensed angiotensin-converting enzyme (ACE) inhibitor and a beta-blocker such as Ramipril with Bisoprolol. All the other options stated are incorrect because rate limiting calcium channel blockers such as Verapamil, Diltiazem and short-acting dihydropyridine agents such as Nifedipine and Nicardipine must be avoided. This is because these drugs further depress cardiac contractility. https://www.nice.org.uk/guidance/n g106/chapter/recommendations#tr eating-heart-failure-with-reduced-ejection-fraction
103.	E	Option E is the correct answer, potassium salt alternatives should not be considered, due to risk of hyperkalaemia. Hyperkalaemia that is left untreated can lead to fatal cardiac arrhythmias, which are abnormal heart rhythms and worsen heart failure also.
104.	C	Option C is the correct answer, this is because a long acting dihydropyridine calcium channel blocker such as Amlodipine does not significantly reduce cardiac contractility. Amlodipine has vasodilator effects without significant negative inotropic properties and has been used safely in patients with congestive heart failure. While, clinically it is also licensed as an antihypertensive and antianginal oral medication. Nifedipine and

		Nicardipine are short acting dihydropyridine CCB's and are associated with haemodynamic worsening of heart failure. Option D is incorrect as Atropine is an anticholinergic licensed to treat symptomatic bradycardia. Option B is also incorrect as Diphenhydramine is an antihistamine drug, thus, no correlation to the therapeutic drug management of this patient. https://www.nice.org.uk/guidance/ng106/chapter/recommendations#heart-failure-with-reduced-ejection-fraction
105.	B	Option B is the correct answer. The patient's heart failure is now worsening which is being displayed as congestive symptoms such as breathlessness, peripheral oedema accumulation and tiredness. Worsening of glycaemic control would not lead in fluid accumulation, so option A is incorrect. If the patient was experiencing a DVT/TIA/clot then the symptoms would be much more severe and prominent with red hot swollen limbs that are painful. Or if the cerebrovascular region is involved then some sort of headache symptom with sudden onset would be present. https://bnf.nice.org.uk/treatment-summary/chronic-heart-failure.html
106.	A	Option B is incorrect, although thiazide diuretics can benefit Mr

		HT, should his renal function be optimum, and he have an eGFR greater than 30 mL/minute/1.73m^2. The dose of 2.5mg OD is only licensed for hypertension, a higher dose of 5-10mg would be required to tackle peripheral oedema. Option C is incorrect as Digoxin is a cardiac glycoside and not primarily indicated for the treatment for oedema in heart failure. Warfarin is a coumarin based anticoagulants therefore not required in this patient. Option E is also incorrect. Although spironolactone is used as a second line treatment to manage resistant oedema. So, a loop diuretic would be recommended.
107.	C	Option A is incorrect as it is a very common extrapyramidal symptom. It is the constant urge to move and feel very restless. Most extrapyramidal symptoms are involuntary. Dystonia is repetitive muscle movement which is also a very common extrapyramidal affect. Option C is the correct answer, coughing is not a commonly associated symptom. Option D and option E are incorrect as they are extrapyramidal symptoms.
108.	A	Option A is the correct answer. The new medicines service (NMS) https://psnc.org.uk/services-commissioning/essential-services/

109.	A	Option A is the correct answer, ocular discharge is not often related to signs of toxicity, it is usually associated with an infection. All the other symptoms stated are correct and can indicate ocular toxicity. https://bnf.nice.org.uk/drug/hydroxychloroquine-sulfate.html
110.	D	Option D is the correct answer, Linagliptin is a DPP4-inhibitor, this agent is not dependent upon renal function and can be given to those with chronic kidney disease. Although Sitagliptin is also a DPP4-inhibitor, the dose must be reduced according to renal function, therefore for this patient if Sitagliptin is prescribed then the dose must carefully be chosen against the declining renal function. All the other drugs not DPP4-Inhibitors, therefore not the correct option. https://bnf.nice.org.uk/drug/linagliptin.html
111.	B	Option B is the correct answer, your job as a pharmacist is to ensure that drugs, doses, and indications are all appropriate for the patient. This appropriateness of this is usually carried out during the drug screening process and medicines reconciliation process. For this patient you must calculate the creatinine clearance to determine renal function. The creatinine clearance is 24ml/min,

		therefore as the extract states, the normal dose of the patient must be halved. For a patient with normal renal function the dose should have been 23mg X 67kg = 1541mg/kg. However, as half of this dose is required then approximately 770.5mg/kg is needed. The doctor has issued a lower dose of 500 mg BD, according to this patient it may be less than effective against the septicaemia. So, an average dose of 750mg BD would be more appropriate and should be recommended to the doctor.
112.	D	Option D is the correct answer, Carbocisteine splits the glycoprotein bonds in mucus, therefore, used as an expectorant mucolytic used in the relief of respiratory congestive disorders. https://bnf.nice.org.uk/drug/carbocisteine.html
113.	B	When starting a patient on a statin, it is very important to ensure that their liver function test is not abnormal. Therefore, option B is correct the hepatic enzymes must be tested for to ensure they are not raised which would indicate hepatic abnormality.
114.	A	Option A is the correct answer, SLS stands for 'selected list scheme' and is a list of products that the drug tariff has listed to only be prescribed against certain

		indications, in specific conditions. A 'Selected List' can be found in Schedule 2 of the NHS (General Medical Services Contracts) (Prescription of Drugs etc.) Regulations 2004. When a prescriber produces a prescription, they must state the specific endorsement (SLS), otherwise if it is missing, then the NHSBSA payment service shall not approve payment appropriately. https://nhsbsa-live.powerappsportals.com/knowledgebase/article/KA-03227/en-us
115.	B	Option B is the correct answer, Oxybutynin has never been used for pain relief. It has always been licensed for symptomatic management of an overactive bladder. The patient is most probably confusing this with a drug of a very similar name, perhaps (Oxycodone). All the other options stated are incorrect because they are false statements. https://bnf.nice.org.uk/drug/oxybutynin-hydrochloride.html
116.	A	Option A is the correct answer, the patient will not have to pay any charge, as contraceptives are free of charge on an NHS prescription. Although. If the item was a regular drug, then she would have been liable for ONE prescription charge. https://psnc.org.uk/dispensing-supply/endorsement/fees-allowances/consumables-

		containers/
117.	B	Option B is the correct answer, as both the medications are the same formulation, with the same active ingredient on the same form, the patient should be charged ONE charge only. https://psnc.org.uk/dispensing-supply/endorsement/fees-allowances/consumables-containers/
118.	B	Option B is the correct. If the patient does not have any exemptions and is not exempt from paying the prescription charge, as both the dry powder for injection and diluent (WFI) has been prescribed on the same prescription form, only one prescription charge should be levied. https://psnc.org.uk/dispensing-supply/endorsement/fees-allowances/consumables-containers/
119.	E	Option E is the correct option, Pizotifen is not a controlled drug.
120.	C	Option C is the correct option. Amorolfine 5% solution is used treat fungal infections and can be sold to be used OTC to anyone over the age of 18 years. There is no evidence base to suggest and support its effectivity in those patients who are aged under the age of 18 years. Thus, you cannot make the sale.

		https://www.medicines.org.uk/emc/product/7414/smpc#gref
121.	E	Option A is incorrect as Estriol is an oestrogen-based cream licensed for females. Option B is incorrect as it is an NSAID based topical gel for pain relief. Both options C and D are incorrect as they steroid based creams. This means option E is the correct answer, it is licensed to treat minor skin malignancies in the community. https://www.medicines.org.uk/emc/product/9260/smpc#gref
122.	D	Option D is the correct answer, Trihexyphenidyl is an anticholinergic drug, a non-selective muscarinic acetylcholine antagonist. It acts to block excess ACH which prevents Parkinsonian symptoms caused by dopamine lowering agents. Option A is the incorrect answer as Primidone changes sodium and calcium channel support, which lowers the seizure potential and tremor potential for patients, but not effective in reducing drug induced extrapyramidal symptoms. All the other options stated are irrelevant. https://bnf.nice.org.uk/drug/trihexyphenidyl-hydrochloride.html
123.	D	Option D is the correct answer. Bladder instability is caused by spontaneous contractions by the destructor muscle, during the filling

		phase in the bladder. As the bladder gradually fills with the urine filtrate, spasmic contractions from the detrusor would often interrupt this and attempt to urinate. Often leading to incomplete, interrupted, and unsatisfactory urination. Oxybutynin would be used to relax the surrounding muscle of the bladder and help with symptom control. https://adc.bmj.com/content/83/2/1 35
124.	A	Option A is the correct answer. Urinary urgency relates to how strongly a person may need to urinate. As urine collects within the bladder, pressure rises, it comes to a point where the person can no longer hold the pressure and they must release the urine out through urination. https://adc.bmj.com/content/83/2/1 35
125.	B	Option B is the correct answer. Urinary frequency relates to how many times a person may need to urinate within a set period. Usually within a 24hr day, a person would need to urinate between 6-7 times, which is healthy. https://www.nhs.uk/conditions/urina ry-incontinence/causes/
126.	C	Option C is the correct answer. Continence is a term which describes the level of self-control and restraint an individual has over

		voluntary urination or defecation. However, when a person becomes incontinent, they then lack that voluntary control, often leading to accidents of wetting themselves or defecating unwillingly. https://www.nhs.uk/conditions/urinary-incontinence/causes/
127.	E	Option E is the correct answer. Micturition is the act if urination, the passing of urine filtrate through a urethra, a natural reflex for the body. https://www.sciencedirect.com/topics/medicine-and-dentistry/micturition-reflex
128.	C	Option C is the correct answer. Post-partum, especially when a female gives birth to a child naturally. Then this physiological strain on the female's genital region can lead to stress incontinence. Usually stress incontinence is only transient and resolves within 6-8 weeks after giving birth. Pelvic floor exercises could be used to help strengthen muscles and assist with the incontinence. Should it become a chronic problem for the patient then she should refer herself for medical assistance. https://www.nhs.uk/conditions/urinary-incontinence/causes/
129.	H	Option H is the correct answer, the patient's symptoms are suggestive of BPH. Research has found that in

		males over the age of 50 years, about 1 in 3 men experience some symptoms because of an enlarged prostate. The BPH causes narrowing of the first part of the urethra, which can obstruct the flow of urine from the bladder, which can precipitate symptoms of urgency or frequency. The fact he has altered/painful ejaculation, is a complication which needs to be investigated. https://www.esht.nhs.uk/wp-content/uploads/2017/06/0392.pdf
130.	D	Option D is the correct answer, Tolterodine is a competitive antagonist of acetylcholine muscarinic receptors. This acts to relax the smooth muscles of the bladder and peripheral detrusor muscles. This then, reduces transient contractions and alleviate associated symptoms. Tamsulosin is incorrect as it is used in those with benign prostatic hyperplasia, and not used for urinary symptoms not associated with BPH. Terlipressin is an intravenous drug, used for the management of bleeding from oesophageal varices. https://bnf.nice.org.uk/drug/tolterodine-tartrate.html
131.	D	Clindamycin is an antibacterial agent; this works primarily by binding to the 50s ribosomal subunit of bacteria. The Clindamycin disrupts protein

		synthesis process by interfering with the translation process reaction. This prevents the bacteria from producing protein which would assist the bacteria to proliferate. https://bnf.nice.org.uk/drug/clindamycin.html#medicinalForms
132.	B	Option B is the correct answer, as a pharmacist alongside apologizing, it is also your priority to identify if the patient was harmed by using the incorrect drug. If the patient did use it, then the National Reporting and Learning System NRLS must be informed, as well as the patients prescriber. Appropriate records should be made of the encounter with the patient and of any action taken. If the patient is harmed or had adverse effects, they immediately should seek medical attention. Option A is not the best action to take as it should be dealt by you at that moment instead of passing it to someone else. Investigating the matter further is fine, but to pass the blame onto a colleague is again not very professional and wouldn't address the patient's level of harm immediately, so option C is incorrect. At this early stage of the scenario, it would be unsuitable to refer the matter to the GPhC without a thorough investigation, and not taken any action/steps to

		help the patient. Option E is also incorrect as Nortriptyline is not indicated for delaying female menstruation, it is only indicated for depression or neuropathic pain. The patient requires Norethisterone. https://bnf.nice.org.uk/drug/nortript yline.html
133.	E	Option E is correct. Nortriptyline inhibits the reuptake of serotonin and norepinephrine by the presynaptic neuronal membrane, thereby increasing the concentration of those neurotransmitters in the synapse. https://www.medicines.or g.uk/emc/product/9968/smpc#gref
134.	A	Norethisterone is what should have been dispensed originally, as it is licensed for delaying female menstruation. It would be given at a dose of 5 mg TDS, from days 5– 26 of the menstrual cycle. https://cks.nice.org.uk/topics/ menorrhagia/prescribing-information/oral-norethisterone/
135.	C	Option C is the correct answer, angiotensin receptor blocker (ARB) drugs such as Losartan acts on the RAAS system, to selectively block the binding of angiotensin to the angiotensin receptors and this causes vascular smooth muscle relaxation, lowering blood pressure. Option A is incorrect as Bisoprolol is an example of a beta-

		blocking agent, option B is in correct as Verapamil is a rate limiting calcium channel blocker. Options D and E are incorrect as they both are examples of alpha blockers. https://www.medicines.org.uk/emc/product/6004/smpc#gref
136.	D	Option D is the correct answer, patients with hypertension do not need to use Sildenafil with caution. All the other options stated are either contraindicated or cautioned with erectile dysfunction medication such as Sildenafil. https://www.medicines.org.uk/emc/product/7141/smpc#gref
137.	D	Option D is the correct answer. Glomerular filtration rate (GFR) represents the flow of plasma from the glomerulus into Bowman's space over a specified period and is the chief measure of kidney function. Usually measured as litres per minute. https://www.kidney.org/atoz/content/gfr
138.	A	Option A is the correct answer, propranolol is a nonselective beta-blocking agent, therefore this may precipitate bronchospasm in patients who suffer from asthma and can increase airway resistance. Although this can be dose dependent. https://www.ncbi.nlm.nih.gov/pmc/articles/PMC5270217/

139.	C	Option C is the correct answer, although option E could be perceived as correct, peripheral oedema is only a symptom of worsening heart failure. Thus, the actual causing condition would be heart failure, as her symptoms suggest, the heart is unable to pump an efficient ejection amount of blood from the ventricles. This can lead to coughing up blood stained or pink, frothy mucus because of pulmonary oedema. The swelling in the lower calf could be associated with a DVT, but the other symptoms that she is experiencing are not suggestive of a DVT, more perhaps of pulmonary embolism. Option A and D are also incorrect, as they are associated with an irregular heartbeat. A coronary occlusion would cause a heart attack. The patient wouldn't be in a conversing state. https://bnf.nice.org.uk/treatment-summary/chronic-heart-failure.html
140.	A	Option A is correct, loop diuretics such as Furosemide are indicated as first line therapy for treating oedema related with heart failure, which would also address symptoms of dyspnoea. Furosemide inhibits the sodium/potassium/chloride transporter in the thick ascending limb of the loop of Henle, therefore reduces accumulation of fluid and lowers cardiac output. A rate

| | | limiting CCB such a Verapamil must be avoided in patient with heart failure, especially with those who have a reduced ejection fraction as it further depresses cardiac contractility which could be fatal. Option C is incorrect as Nicorandil is not licensed to manage heart failure/oedema. It is a potassium channel activator that dilates blood vessels, licensed for stable angina. Although Spironolactone a (aldosterone antagonist) or Hydralazine (potent vasodilator) could be used in this patient, they both are not indicated as first-line treatments, reserved as second line agents. So, option D and E are also incorrect. It should note that diuretics should be routinely used for the relief of congestive symptoms and fluid retention in people with heart failure, the dose is very carefully titrated to minimise the risk of dehydration, renal impairment, or hypotension, according to response upon initiation. https://bnf.nice.org.uk/treatment-summary/chronic-heart-failure.html |
| **141.** | D | Option A is incorrect, Chloramphenicol is licensed for bacterial conjunctivitis, and shingles is of viral origin so this would be inappropriate. Option B is also incorrect, sensitive regions such as the eyes must only be bathed with an appropriate eye |

		wash solutions not any antiviral solution. Most antiviral eye drops solutions are prescription only medications, so signposting to a different pharmacy would only waste the patient's time. Sending the patient back home would also endanger the patient as his shingles could be complicated especially if the optical region is included, so option E is incorrect. Option D is correct.
142.	B	Option B is the correct answer, Doxycycline can cause photosensitivity reactions. As prolonged exposure to UV rays or sunlight can cause irritation, rashes, itching, redness, discolouration, or a burn. While the patient is taking a tetracycline it is advised to keep the skin covered as much as possible, when in a sun lit environment. https://www.medicines.org.uk/emc/product/4063/smpc#gref
143.	A	Option A is the correct answer, metformin is commonly associated with causing taste disturbance in the patient. Some patients who are on regular metformin therapy describe their taste as becoming metallic, this is due to the Metformin being present in the salivary glands. https://bnf.nice.org.uk/drug/metformin-hydrochloride.html

144.	C	Option C is the correct answer, Microgynon 30® is a combined oral contraceptive which has synthetic oestrogen and progesterone. With this medication, it can make the blood more viscid which increases the probability of developing a blood clot. Most common forms of blood clots are DVT's and pulmonary embolisms. Asthma is not an associated side effect of contraceptives. All the other options are incorrect as they are malignancies not associated with a Microgynon 30®. https://www.medicines.org.uk/emc/product/1130/smpc#gref
145.	E	Option E is the correct answer. Typical signs of respiratory depression include day-time sleepiness, tiredness, headaches, and peripheral cyanosis cause by CO_2 accumulation. Healthcare professionals must note that respiratory depression is very commonly associated with Methadone hydrochloride administration. As typical respiratory depressant effects typically occur after the plasma Methadone levels exert their peak analgesic effects. Option A is incorrect, as the patient has not consumed alcohol for a prolonged period, therefore the chances of her experiencing alcohol withdrawal is minimal. Option B, D would be inappropriate for the

		patient, as it would mask an underlying condition, even though sleep hygiene advice would help, it is important to address the cause of her symptoms. Option C is also not appropriate, this is because the patient has already informed you that her recent blood investigations were in range. https://www.fda.gov/media/76020/d ownload#:~:text=Respiratory%20d epression%20is%20the%20chief,in %20the%20early%20dosing%20pe riod https://www.nhs.uk/conditions/acut e-respiratory-distress-syndrome
146.	E	Option E is the correct answer. Even recent safety reports have stated that boric acid must be used cautiously in the patient population under the age of 2 years. However, a typical regimen of one drop, applied typically 3 to 4 times a day, to both eyes, would result in a low exposure, below the safety limit for children aged 0 to 2 years. Chloramphenicol eye drops containing borax or boric acid buffers: use in children younger than 2 years - GOV.UK (www.gov.uk)
147.	B	Option B is the correct answer. The patient is most likely to be experiencing symptoms of digoxin toxicity. The symptoms the patient has presented with such as visual changes, confusion and nausea are commonly related to digoxin

		accumulation which causes toxicity and induces hyperkalaemia. Blockage of the sodium/potassium ATPase pump results in higher serum potassium levels. The patient's plasma digoxin levels need to be investigated. https://bnf.nice.org.uk /drug/digoxin.html
148.	B	Option B is the correct answer, when selling Co-Codamol 8/500mg tablets, no more than 32 tablets could be sold legally under the same transaction to one patient, due to the risk of addiction. https://www.gov.uk/drug-safety-update/over-the-counter-painkillers-containing-codeine-or-dihydrocodeine
149.	E	Option E is the correct answer, Chlorphenamine in a sedative antihistamine. All the other drugs stated are not associated with drowsiness. https://bnf.nice.org.uk/drug/chlorph enamine-maleate.html
150.	D	Option D is the correct answer, hyponatraemia is a serious, complication of diuretic therapy. Loop diuretics are more common to cause hyponatremia. This is because loop diuretics inhibit the sodium transport in the renal medulla and prevent the generation of an osmotic gradient. This then impairs the urinary concentrating ability and

		precipitates hyponatraemia. https://bnf.nice.org.uk/drug/furose mide.html
151.	C	Option C is the correct answer, public transport as a whole is not classed as a trigger factor for migraines. Although there may be certain factors within public transport like; lack of fresh air, lights or smells that can trigger migraines, but not public transport generally. All the other options stated are clinically suggestive of triggering migraines. https://www.nhs.uk/conditions/migr aine/causes/
152.	B	Option B is the correct answer, Amitriptyline is an anticholinergic agent which can cause the affects that he has been experiencing. Amitriptyline is known to increase noradrenergic or serotonergic neurotransmission by blockage of the norepinephrine or serotonin transporter. This can further cause anticholinergic effects. https://www.medicines.org.uk/emc/ product/5698/smpc#gref
153.	C	Option C is the correct answer. Liraglutide is the incorrect option because it activates the Glucagon-Like-Peptide-1, it acts to increase pancreatic insulin secretion. It does not have any renal action. Sitagliptin is a DPP4-inhibitor which also acts to increase insulin secretion and lower levels of

		glucagon. Biguanide is also the incorrect option as it basically is the class for Metformin which the patient already tolerates well. Lisinopril is not an antidiabetic medication so not applicable in this scenario. Dapagliflozin is the correct answer, this is because it is a reversible inhibitor of the sodium-glucose co-transporter 2 (SGLT2) within the renal proximal convoluted tubule. This acts to reduce glucose reabsorption and increases urinary glucose excretion, thus causing the patients unwanted urinary symptoms. https://bnf.nice.org.uk/drug/dapagliflozin.html
154.	C	Option C is the correct answer, as the patient already is morbidly obese, he should not be given any agent that would promote further weight gain. https://bnf.nice.org.uk/drug/gliclazide.html
155.	A	Option A is the best option to take, as the patient has been experiencing a higher frequency of urination with the SGLT-2 inhibitor, it should be replaced by an alternative and trialled for some period, then his HbA1C should be reassessed to see if any improvement has been made in his diabetic control. Option B is not correct as giving the patient an alternative SGLT-2 inhibitor would not solve his issue. Option C is an

		unlicensed dose and not recommended. Options D and E are not providing patient centred care, and are not helping the patient to manage his diabetes better. https://www.nice.org.uk/guidance/ng28

Simple Pharmacy Question Answers

1.	Indicated for major depression. https://bnf.nice.org.uk/drug/agomelatine.html
2.	Intracavernosal injections are a treatment option for ED where you inject drugs into the spongy tissue, in the penis to open the blood vessels. https://www.medicines.org.uk/emc/product/2917/smpc#gref
3.	Indicated primarily for erectile dysfunction in males. https://bnf.nice.org.uk/drug/alprostadil.html
4.	Amantadine is a weak antagonist of the NMDA-type glutamate receptor, increases dopamine release, and blocks dopamine reuptake. https://www.medicines.org.uk/emc#gref
5.	Yes, Aminophylline is licensed as oral modified release tablets or as an intravenous injection. https://bnf.nice.org.uk/medicinal-forms/aminophylline.html
6.	Yes, Amoxicillin is safe to take by pregnant patients. There is limited data that indicate a risk of congenital malformations, therefore safe to take. https://www.medicines.org.uk/emc/product/526/smpc#gref
7.	Anastrazole has been associated to have a common side effect of causing alopecia.

	Anastrozole lowers oestrogen levels by preventing the synthesis of oestrogen from adrenal androgens. https://www.medicines.org.uk/emc/product/2749/smpc
8.	Yes, most licensed Ascorbic acid (vitamin C) products can be taken from the age of 6 months and above. https://www.nhs.uk/conditions/baby/weaning-and-feeding/vitamins-for-children/
9.	Azithromycin is a macrolide antibiotic. Macrolide antibiotics such as Azithromycin bind the bacterial 50S ribosomal subunits, which disrupt bacterial protein synthesis and help fight the infection, preventing proliferation. https://www.ncbi.nlm.nih.gov/pmc/articles/PMC2901655/
10.	Atenolol is more water soluble, therefore it is less likely to enter the brain, and may perhaps cause less sleep disturbance and nightmares. https://bnf.nice.org.uk/treatment-summary/beta-adrenoceptor-blocking-drugs.html
11.	Propranolol is licensed as an adjunct in Thyrotoxicosis. https://bnf.nice.org.uk/drug/propranolol-hydrochloride.html
12.	Aldosterone has a homeostatic control within the body. It acts to reabsorb water and salt back into the blood stream. It primarily acts on the mineralocorticoid receptors in the distal tubules and collecting ducts of the nephron. https://www.hormone.org/your-health-and-hormones/glands-and-hormones-a-to-z/hormones/aldosterone
13.	The kidneys are primarily responsible for producing and activating Erythropoietin within the

	body to regulate RBC production. Less Erythropoietin can cause blood anaemia. https://www.hormone.org/your-health-and-hormones/glands-and-hormones-a-to-z/hormones/erythropoietin
14.	No, Proguanil is taken daily. Usually, to be started 1 week before travelling and stopped 4 weeks after travelling. https://bnf.nice.org.uk/drug/proguanil-hydrochloride.html
15.	A DEXA scan stands for Dual-energy X-Ray Absorptiometry. It is used to measure bone mineral density using spectral image data. Often used in the management and diagnosis of osteoporosis. https://www.nhs.uk/conditions/dexa-scan/what-happens/
16.	When Pioglitazone is used concomitantly with insulin, the patient is at an increased risk of developing heart failure, evidence suggests that this combination as anti-diabetic therapy should be avoided in patients. https://bnf.nice.org.uk/drug/pioglitazone.html
17.	The patient must be informed to have adequate contraception, during the treatment with the statin and for 1 month afterwards also. This is because statins interfere with foetal development. https://bnf.nice.org.uk/drug/simvastatin.html
18.	Donepezil is a reversible inhibitor of acetylcholinesterase. This inhibits the hydrolysis of acetylcholine at the synapses and increases its availability. https://bnf.nice.org.uk/drug/donepezil-hydrochloride.html
19.	A Rivastigmine patch is replaced every 24 hours.

	These patches are for daily dosing there are two common strengths licensed for the patch, either as a 4.6☐mg/24☐hours patch or a 9.5☐mg/24 hours patch. https://bnf.nice.org.uk/drug/rivastigmine.html#dire ctionsForAdministration
20.	The patient must be reminded that when a patient changes a patch, they must apply the replacement patch to a different area. The patient should avoid using the same area for at least 2 weeks. https://bnf.nice.org.uk/drug/rivastigmine.html#dire ctionsForAdministration
21.	The patient must be informed that evidence has shown, Rifampicin tends to colour soft ocular contact lenses. So, the patient must be advised to avoid wearing contact lenses during the period of the treatment. Furthermore, the staining may also extend to the colour of the urine, saliva, tears, and other bodily fluid secretions to stain an Orange to red colour. https://www.medicines.org.uk/emc/product/8789/s mpc#gref
22.	Leukopenia is a condition in which there is a decrease in the availability of active white blood cells. Thus, lowers immunity and increases the persons chances to get an infection.
23.	NSAIDs reduce renal perfusion of blood and tends to lower renal clearance. As a result, this will lower the urinary excretion of the excess calcium and perhaps worsen the hypercalcaemia, which may further precipitate atrial fibrillation. A weak opioid may be better suited. https://cks.nice.org.uk/topics/hypercalcaemia/diag nosis/assessment/
24.	Dysuria is not a commonly associated symptom

	of dehydration. Usually, it is a sign of a UTI, which is serious in males and warrants referral, therefore. Advice the female to get her father seen by a medical professional. https://bnf.nice.org.uk/treatment-summary/fluids-and-electrolytes.html
25.	Warfarin is a vitamin K antagonist. Therefore, increasing dietary vitamin K has been associated with thickening of the blood, which results in a lower INR reading.
26.	'Nulliparous' is a medical term which describes a female patient who has not given birth to any child yet. She may be sexually active, but she has not given birth.
27.	Women who are managed on Methyldopa as an antihypertensive during their pregnancy must stop within 2 days after giving birth. Should she require an antihypertensive, then she should be given an alternative. This is because Methyldopa tends to increase the chances of post-natal depression, so must be avoided.
28.	Trimethoprim is an antibiotic which is acutely used to treat urinate tract infections. Trimethoprim is a folate antagonist, and during pregnancy especially the first trimester, folic acid is vital for foetal development. So, Trimethoprim should be avoided.
29.	Currently Canagliflozin and Empagliflozin are not licensed for heart failure, however, Dapagliflozin is the only SGLT-2 inhibitor for symptomatic chronic heart failure with reduced ejection fraction. https://bnf.nice.org.uk/drug/dapagliflozin.html. https://www.acc.org/latest-in-cardiology/clinical-trials/2019/08/30/21/33/dapa-hf

30.	Flucloxacillin is an oral penicillin-based antibiotic, which can be used by both adults and children, the pharmacy team must convey the following counselling points - to complete the course as instructed by prescriber as this is an antibiotic. To space the doses over the day evenly. The medicine must ideally be taken at least 1 hour before or 2 hours after meals, for optimum absorption. https://www.medicines.org.uk/emc/files/pil.545.pdf
31.	Within clinical practise, anticoagulation may have unpredictable effects, especially during invasive procedures. Unfractionated heparins have the advantage of having short activity and reversibility. In comparison to LMWH, they stay in the plasma for longer due to their ability to bind less to plasma proteins, therefore, LMWH have increased bioavailability and duration of action. https://bnf.nice.org.uk/treatment-summary/parenteral-anticoagulants.html
32.	Malaena is a medical term to describe a patient experiencing black/tarry stools. This is usually caused by an internal gastrointestinal bleed, which would require a referral for medical examination.
33.	Inform the patient that the Prednisolone is a steroid tablet that must be taken in the morning. Best taken in the morning because it would mimic the body's own production of cortisone. Evidence has suggested that taking the dose of Prednisolone later in the day or before going to bed may cause insomnia as the altered inflammatory cytokine release caused by Prednisolone can disrupt sleep. https://www.medicines.org.uk/emc/product/2427/smpc#gref

34.	The dose is 150 mg 3 times a day, or a maximum 30 mg/kg per day. https://bnf.nice.org.uk/drug/ibuprofen.htm
35.	The dose is 1 mg every 4–6 hours or a maximum of 6 mg per day. https://bnf.nice.org.uk/drug/chlorphenamine-maleate.htm
36.	After taking an immediate dose of Levonorgestrel, exposure of the drug to her daughter can be minimized by avoiding breast-feeding her for at least 8 hours after the dose. Milk can be expressed and discarded in this period. https://www.medicines.org.uk/emc/product/7308/smpc#gref
37.	Women who are obese and have a BMI ≥ 30 kg/m² are prone to have altered pharmacokinetics and distribution across the body. Studies have showed that such patients are at risk of pregnancy as the plasma concentrations of Levonorgestrel are lower with a 1.5mg dose. Such patients would benefit from a 3mg dose. However, two 1.5mg doses cannot be sold OTC, to make a total dose of 3mg. So, she should be referred to her GP or sexual health clinic to get it prescribed. https://www.medicines.org.uk/emc/product/7308/smpc#gref
38.	It is a type of review, which has a purpose to optimise medication usage for patients. It may involve de-prescribing, changing medications, regimens, and appropriate counselling. https://www.nice.org.uk/guidance/qs120/chapter/quality-statement-6-structured-medication-review
39.	You as the pharmacist have a duty of candour, professionals are required to speak up when they have concerns or when things go wrong.

	Although several other standards would also apply in this scenario. Standard 8 is primarily demonstrated through this. Https://www.pharmacyregulation.org/sites/default/files/standards_for_pharmacy_professionals_may_2017_0.pdf
40.	Loop diuretics such as Furosemide are known to inhibit lactation in post gestational women. Therefore, they are best avoided. https://bnf.nice.org.uk/drug/furosemide.html#breastfeeding
41.	Ezetimibe is a potent and inhibitor of intestinal cholesterol absorption. This then reduces overall delivery of cholesterol to the hepatic regions and aim to lower LDL levels. https://www.medicines.org.uk/emc/product/9109/smpc#gref
42.	Lacosamide is a MHRA category 3 drug, so it would be unnecessary for the pharmacist to ensure that Miss GT is maintained on a specific manufacturer's brand. Thus, you could supply the emergency supply of a different brand safely. https://www.gov.uk/drug-safety-update/antiepileptic-drugs-new-advice-on-switching-between-different-manufacturers-products-for-a-particular-drug
43.	In a female's lifetime, the ceasing of menstruation is primarily classed as menopause. When menopause approaches, the ovary in the female produces significantly less oestrogen, this gradual decrease eventually stops periods, and the female body then has to adapt to physical changes due to the altered hormone levels. Post-menopausal women cannot conceive post-coitus. https://www.nhs.uk/conditions/menopause/

44.	Sildenafil is used for managing episodes of erectile dysfunction in males. Nonetheless, Sildenafil is also licensed for pulmonary arterial hypertension and digital ulceration. So, Mrs DW may have a different indication for why she has been prescribed Sildenafil. https://bnf.nice.org.uk/drug/sildenafil.html
45.	For this patient, Pioglitazone is a new medication, her dark urine could potentially be a sign of her Pioglitazone causing hepatic toxicity. You must not sell the cystitis treatment as it may mask the underlying cause and she must seek immediate medical attention for further investigation. Other symptoms of hepatic toxicity include feeling nauseous, vomiting, abdominal pain, fatigue, and dark urine. https://bnf.nice.org.uk/drug/pioglitazone.html
46.	Acarbose is indicated in those patients who have poorly controlled diabetes. It delays the intestinal digestion and absorption of starch and sucrose, therefore assisted to manage plasma glucose levels better. https://bnf.nice.org.uk/drug/acarbose.html#indicationsAndDoses
47.	The patient must be counselled appropriately on how to take Acarbose, inform them that according to the manufacturer's advice, Acarbose tablets should be chewed with the first mouthful of food. If this is not ideal for the patient, then tablets must be swallowed whole with a little liquid immediately before any food is consumed. https://bnf.nice.org.uk/drug/acarbose.html#indicationsAndDoses. https://www.medicines.org.uk/emc/product/10000/smpc#gref
48.	The EEA stands for the European Economic Area. https://www.gov.uk/guidance/prescriptions-

	issued-in-the-eea-and-switzerland-guidance-for-pharmacists
49.	Finasteride is a 5-alpha-reductase inhibitor. This inhibition prevents the transformation of testosterone to dihydrotestosterone (DHT). In males, DHT is primarily responsible for the androgen action within the testes for males. Finasteride does have anti-androgen activity. https://www.medicines.org.uk/emc/product/547/smpc#gref
50.	Rotigotine is a dopamine-receptor agonist that is associated with impulse control disorders, including pathological gambling, binge eating, and hyper sexuality. Daytime sudden onset of sleepiness is commonly associated with dopamine-receptor agonists. Patients starting treatment with these drugs should be warned of the risk and of the need to exercise caution when driving or operating machinery. https://bnf.nice.org.uk/drug/rotigotine.html
51.	Norethisterone is a synthetic analogue that mimics endogenous progesterone, but of a higher efficacy. It acts on endometrial function to alter menstruation. The female patient must take it three days before menstruation, then usually to continue for up to 20 days for total treatment. This will delay the period, then bleeding should commence soon after. https://www.medicines.org.uk/emc/product/1494/smpc#gref
52.	This female is showing signs of an upper gastrointestinal bleed. Most probably the NSAID is causing. Symptoms of internal bleeding from NSAIDs include blood in your stool, severe abdominal pain, vomiting blood and tarry stools. https://bnf.nice.org.uk/treatment-summary/non-steroidal-anti-inflammatory-drugs.html

53.	Repaglinide is a secretagogue that promotes insulin release from β-islet cells of the pancreas licensed for managing diabetes mellitus Type-2 as mono therapy or as an adjunct. https://bnf.nice.org.uk/drug/repaglinide.html
54.	Within the care setting, syringe drivers are very common, they provide medicines for symptom management in patients who are terminally ill. They allow continuous subcutaneous administration of medicines to enable effective symptom control when medicines given by other routes are inappropriate or no longer effective. https://www.mariecurie.org.uk/help/support/terminal-illness/medication-pain-relief/syringe-drivers

Yes / No Question Answers

1.	No	Risedronate 35 mg doses are taken weekly, but Risedronate 5mg doses are taken daily. https://bnf.nice.org.uk/drug/risedronate-sodium.html
2.	No	The BBB is primarily a lipid barrier; therefore, a more hydrophobic molecule would diffuse across the membranes of the BBB, due to their lipid soluble nature. Nonetheless, the molecule must still have a small percentage of hydrophilicity to navigate through the brain's cavity.
3.	No	Dermatitis is characterised by the irritation of the focal skin layer, usually precipitating an allergic reaction. Koplik spots are only associated with Measles, not dermatitis. Koplik spots are small, often pale/white coloured spots

		that develop on the oral mucosa on the inside of the mouth early on with Measles.
4.	No	She should not use any eye preparation that is intended to be used multiple times for more than 4 weeks after first opening, unless the manufacturer instructs otherwise. https://bnf.nice.org.uk/treatment-summary/eye.html
5.	No	Evidence suggests that Ulipristal acetate does not interrupt an existing pregnancy, however, it is advised not to take it should the patient suspect they are currently pregnant. https://www.medicines.org.uk/emc/product/6657/smpc#gref
6.	Yes	Malarone® must be commenced 24 or 48 hours prior to entering a malaria-endemic area, to provide adequate protection. https://www.medicines.org.uk/emc/product/947/smpc#gref
7.	Yes	Having an eGFR between 15-28ml/min/1.73m^2 indicates stage 4 renal disease, 'severely reduced kidney function'. https://ukidney.com/nephrology-resources/egfr-calculator
8.	No	Nebulised salbutamol causes hypokalaemia and is used to treat hyperkalaemia as a potassium lowering agent. The patient's cardiac function and ECG may

		need to be monitored. https://bnf.nice.org.uk/drug/salbutamol.html
9.	Yes	Fluoroquinolones are a class of antibiotics that are used to manage bacterial infections, drugs include Ciprofloxacin, Levofloxacin etc. The Fluoroquinolone antibiotics should be discontinued if the patient experiences any sort of joint pain, unexpected swelling or inflammation which would be a sign of tendon damage. In such cases the medication usage should be ceased. https://bnf.nice.org.uk/treatment-summary/quinolones.html
10.	No	Amlodipine is contraindicated in breast feeding females. If she must use Amlodipine, then the milk must be expressed but not breast fed. https://bnf.nice.org.uk/drug/amlodipine.html
11	Yes	Levonorgestrel is licensed to be sold under the supervision of a trained pharmacist if the sale and supply is suitable for the patient after a comprehensive consultation. Usually, local PGD's require patients under the age of 16 years to take it under medical supervision. https://www.medicines.org.uk/emc/product/7308/smpc#gref
12	No	This will not be the case, if the patient is already pregnant, taking Levonorgestrel will not interrupt her

		pregnancy at a STAT dose of 1.5mg. https://www.medicines.org.uk/emc/product/7308/smpc#gref
13	No	The statement is incorrect, this is because duty of candour is a requirement for pharmacy professionals to be open and honest, and to speak up when something goes wrong with a patient's treatment, or something needs reporting. https://www.pharmacyregulation.org/sites/default/files/standards_for_pharmacy_professionals_may_2017_0.pdf
14	No	No, Hyoscine Butylbromide is not indicated for this, due to its anticholinergic action smooth muscle it will be ineffective in helping to manage ulceration. Instead, the anti-spasmodic effect and blockage of muscarinic receptors in the gastrointestinal is useful in managing IBS, cramping, spasms, and excessive respiratory tract secretions. https://bnf.nice.org.uk/drug/hyoscine-butylbromide.html
15.	No	This is incorrect as Phenytoin is classed as a MHRA Category 1 drug. So, a patient must be maintained on a specific manufacturer's brand. So only one brand (if had before then that same one) should be dispensed, if so gain further clarification from the

		prescriber and patient. https://www.gov.uk/drug-safety-update/antiepileptic-drugs-new-advice-on-switching-between-different-manufacturers-products-for-a-particular-drug
16.	No	This is false, even though bacterial conjunctivitis can be treated with Chloramphenicol OTC, any association of pain in the eye warrants immediate referral. Pain is classed as a red alarms symptom, there could be a more sinister underlying cause that needs to be addressed first before an OTC treatment is supplied as it could mask it. https://www.england.nhs.uk/wp-content/uploads/2018/05/over-the-counter-quick-reference-guide.pdf
17.	No	This statement is false, Fenofibrate acts by lowering plasma serum triglycerides; and potentially lower low-density-lipoproteins. https://bnf.nice.org.uk/drug/fenofibrate.html
18.	No	This statement is false, Nifedipine is not licensed for heart failure, in terms of cardiovascular disease it is only licensed for hypertension, angina or Reynaud's disease. https://bnf.nice.org.uk/drug/nifedipine.html
19.	No	This statement is false. Solifenacin is not licensed for BPH at all, it is licensed for managing urinary incontinence, urgency, and

		frequency, and it works by relaxing the smooth muscle of the bladder. https://bnf.nice.org.uk/drug/solifenacin-succinate.html
20.	Yes	Clonidine is licensed to prevent vascular and recurrent migraines by lowering intracranial pressure. https://bnf.nice.org.uk/drug/clonidine-hydrochloride.html#indicationsAndDoses
21.	No	This is false, Perampanel is a MHRA category 2 drug, therefore ideally there needs to be a continuous supply of a particular brand. Should the same brand not be maintained then you may need to confirm with the prescriber for clinical advice before switching brands. However, category 2 drugs are not entirely banned from brand switching. The parameters that need to be considered for whether a brand switch is appropriate or not depends on the actual patient, their tolerance and seizure control. https://www.gov.uk/drug-safety-update/antiepileptic-drugs-updated-advice-on-switching-between-different-manufacturers-products
22.	Yes	Alendronic acid 10mg tablets can be taken daily, under the following indications. Such as preventing or treating corticosteroid-induced osteoporosis or osteoporosis in males.

		https://bnf.nice.org.uk/drug/alendro nic-acid.html